Sacred Challenge

Blazing a New Path for the Sunday School of the Future

MIKE RATLIFF

DISCIPLESHIP RESOURCES

P.O. BOX 340003 • NASHVILLE, TN 37203-0003
www.discipleshipresources.org

Cover design by Nanci Lamar.
Interior design and text composition by PerfecType, Nashville, TN.

ISBN 0-88177-479-0

Library of Congress Control Number 2005934553

CONTENTS

INTRODUCTION

I can't say I remember any one particular Sunday school lesson or activity from my childhood. It's not because I didn't go. Even if my parents didn't go to church, my brother and sisters and I always went to Sunday school. We went to a variety of Sunday schools throughout our growing years. Mostly, they were Methodist. We had a history of Methodism in the family, and that's where we usually went when we moved somewhere. One year, we went to Sunday school in a Southern Baptist church in a small Georgia community. There, we learned all the things you were supposed to learn in Sunday school. By the end of that year, I knew the major stories of the Bible, a lot about Jesus, and a smattering of other topics and subjects.

My favorite time in Sunday school, though, was when we went to visit our grandmother, Big Mom, in Waresboro, Georgia. We always went to a little Methodist Church in the community. Going to church meant going to Sunday school and the 11:00 worship service that followed. Sunday school at Waresboro Methodist Church (later it became Waresboro United Methodist) always started out the same way: Everyone met in the church (we never called it the sanctuary) for the Sunday school assembly. The Sunday school superintendent was in charge and we were all welcomed, especially those who were visiting. We sang a couple of hymns, heard the announcements and anything else the superintendent thought we should know, and then we had a prayer. I remember the prayer being long—really long. As a teenager, I remember timing it just to see how long it actually was! I've long forgotten just how long it actually was, but I'll never forget trying to stay still and silent for the duration.

Finally, the "Amen" was declared and we were off to our classes. I joined the small but rowdy elementary group headed to the corner room behind the piano at the front of the church. As I reached the door, I was immediately enveloped in the loving bosom of the grade school teacher, Josephine Spence. Not one child got into the classroom without her signature greeting, that loving hug and, "Hello, Mike, I'm so glad to see you today!" This was spoken in a way that left no doubt. She really did mean it, and she loved every second of being with you as a pupil in her class. I can remember her sweet perfume, liberally applied and then transferred through her greeting ritual to each and every one of her students. What I learned walking into her room was that I was loved. Even as a third grader, I began to understand God's love through one of God's beloved Sunday school teachers. I wanted to be there because I was wanted there. Someone knew my name and loved me for who I was. What better lesson could I expect from Sunday school?

Later, having moved to the family's hometown, I attended this same little church through junior high and high school. I was to learn another lesson from my teacher, Mrs. Spence. I was a teen, and there was no one to teach the youth class. There were six of us on a good Sunday morning, but we still needed a teacher. After much debate, but no progress in finding a volunteer willing to take on the task (I'm not sure what happened to the teacher before her), Josephine spoke up and said, "I'll do it!" I remember that year with Mrs. Spence, once again my teacher, sitting on the front porch or in the living room of the parsonage next to the church holding class.

As I said earlier, I'm really not sure of the content she taught us, but I learned what it means to take responsibility as a leader. I learned about being committed to my faith and church through her. I continued to experience God's love through those consuming hugs.

I had no idea I was a part of something that had been around for well over two hundred years. I didn't know that I had joined an endless parade of people who have been finding meaning on Sunday mornings as they entered the doors of the Sunday school. It was much later when I recognized myself as a participant in that parade of God's people garnering lessons—some intended, and some implied—from its leaders.

Sunday school is on the death list of many in today's church. It is seen as an institution that's function has been served and that's time is rapidly coming to an end. If you look at the numbers, many will agree that they support this thinking. So, why write this book? Why prolong the inevitable?

Maybe we aren't seeing the whole picture. Maybe there is more to this movement than we have been willing to acknowledge. Maybe there is new life just waiting to emerge from unsuspecting rooms where children, youth, and adults are learning lessons not provided in other venues. Could it be that the effectiveness of the Sunday school in the years to come is more about living our faith in effective ways, than it is about our identifying, quantifying, and stratifying the Sunday school as it was or is?

I invite you to join me on a journey that is about discovery. Together, we will discover where this all started and how we got to where we are. Looking to the future, we'll imagine new ways to transform the structure of this institution into a new, organic framework for ministry. This ministry will embrace what has been transformative about Sunday school, and "re-wire" it for a future that grows faithful disciples of Jesus Christ.

1

A Glorious History

Jacob and John were on the run again. They really weren't bad kids, they simply didn't have anything better to do with their time. So they found themselves running through the back alleys of Gloucester, causing all manner of havoc this Sunday, the same as every Sunday they could recall. They felt trapped, like most children their age, in the low-paying jobs of the local pin factory. There was really no choice about whether to work—if you wanted to eat, you worked. They worked long hours, six days a week, in one of the many factories that supported the wealthy class of late eighteenth century England. Because they were without parents and wards of society, there was nowhere to be and no one to be with on Sunday. They spent their free day hunting ways to amuse themselves. Unfortunately for the residents of this small town in the heart of

England, that sometimes meant Jacob and John's amusement was at their expense. The plight of these two young men, and many others in the same situation, had not gone unnoticed. Actually, they and others in their circumstances provided a fairly loud testimony to their presence in the community through their activity around town.

"Those miserable factory mice are at it again!" exclaimed the wife of one of the men of means in Gloucester. She happened to look out the kitchen window just in time to see Jacob and John hop the wall after tramping through her revered flower garden. Her deafening screeches through the window sent the boys skittering around the corner, laughing all the way.

In his role as the publisher of the *Journal*, Gloucester's local paper, Robert Raikes undoubtedly heard the cry for civility from the established leaders of the community. This, connected with his perception of crime as an outcome of ignorance, inspired him to hire a teacher and begin a "Sunday school" for the likes of Jacob and John.

There is some debate about who actually began a program for teaching the children of poverty on Sundays when there was no work. There is also discussion about the motivation. Was this a noble gesture with the interest of the children at heart, or were community leaders seeking a solution to the antics of unruly children, loosed upon communities rushing headlong into the industrial revolution?

Various others in England had made attempts. Even in America, stories of schools providing instruction in scriptures for children on Sundays date back to 1669. However, there was nothing like the organized movement that began with Raikes' school in Gloucester. This effort multiplied into more than one thousand schools by 1795 (Columbia Electronic Encyclopedia, http://www .bartleby.com/65/su/Sundaysc.html, Colombia Electronic Encyclopedia, 6th Edition, Columbia University Press).

Jacob and John soon spent their Sundays learning to read and memorizing scripture. Their antics no longer threatened the peaceful Sunday afternoons for the genteel residents of Gloucester and the surrounding countryside.

The Sunday school movement provided the means for children of no means to learn. Class offerings expanded with the addition of math classes on Saturdays for those children who had the luxury of attending. Sunday schools in America mirrored those in England, becoming the forerunners of public education for those children whose parents were not able to afford the extravagance of private schooling.

Over the past two centuries, the Sunday school has mutated into its current state of being. Gone are the days of sweatshops, where children toiled their days away creating wealth for the factory owners. There are no longer government organizations responsible for the welfare of children who would allow such organized abuse. Public schools and fundamental education are seen as a civic responsibility for most of the civilized world and they no longer rely on the benevolence of the upper class.

Today's Sunday school is a far cry from the initial one, at least in purpose. Some might question whether the current Sunday school actually has a purpose. Through the last two centuries, significant variations of the original idea have presented us with a quite different understanding of what the Sunday school is and should be. While some sing the praises of its legacy, and some continue to see it grow in their situations, there are those who have written an epitaph for the whole idea:

"Here lies the Sunday School. It has had a long and glorious history, but it has been laid to rest in favor of new ways."

Has the Sunday school outlived its usefulness? Is there any life left in religious education for all ages on Sunday mornings? Professionals and laity alike have answers that run the gamut, from undying support to unwavering skepticism.

In *Sacred Challenge*, we will seek to look at the Sunday school in light of its development and its current place in a comprehensive ministry of education in the church. My hope for you, as teachers and leaders, is that you discover new insights for effective ministry through the framework that has evolved in your situation, or find tools for developing a new framework for a revision of the Sunday school in your setting.

Thoughts Along the Path

Most chapters will conclude with "Thoughts Along the Path." It is hoped that through review and reflection, this section can become a useful tool for strengthening and transforming the Sunday school in your church.

What has your experience of Sunday school been?

How has it evolved over the time you have been involved?

What do you think about how or if this institution should be in your current situation?

2

Naming the Challenges

Contemporary Sunday school faces many challenges. For some, those challenges are overwhelming and, in light of the seemingly insurmountable obstacles, they have chosen to throw in the towel. They have pronounced Sunday school dead in the water and are looking elsewhere for models to provide foundational Christian education. In the minds of these naysayers, we have moved to a new place in our history as a church, especially the American church, and must create new and different structures for learning. While there is truth in the observation that cultural shifts are challenging Sunday school as we know it, perhaps there is light yet to be found through diligent discernment of the direction God is calling us.

Sunday School—The Name

There are those who feel the name "Sunday school" has outlived its usefulness. There is a stigma related to the name. For children and youth, it connects with those five days in classrooms most weeks of the year. Getting up one more morning of the week to go to another "school" seems cruel and unusual punishment for some. This creates a barrier even before those children and youth step inside the door of our Sunday schools to experience what we have to offer.

For some adults, it is a reminder of earlier experiences that have shaped who they are today. Here is a story as told by Ms. Ray Roberts:

Granny Bowen was my Sunday school teacher back in Bowman, Georgia. When I was ten years old, Granny taught this class of girls. Granny wasn't her real name, but everybody in Bowman called her Granny. I heard my mother say her name was Hattie, but even my mother wasn't sure. Granny didn't go to seminary. I'm fairly certain she didn't go to college. Given the time and place, she may not have graduated from high school.

Granny didn't know the latest Christian education techniques of the day. Granny never used audio-visuals, which in those days were 16mm film and filmstrips. But every Sunday Granny was there, teaching a class of little girls. And every Sunday before we left, she would hug each of us, kiss us, and tell us that she loved us. She told us that next Sunday she might not be back because she would be going to be with the Lord very soon. Yet every Sunday, Granny was back teaching our class.

I don't remember a particular Bible lesson that she taught. However, somewhere along the way I learned a great deal about the Bible and being a disciple of Christ. Most of all I learned that what matters is faithfulness and showing our love. It is more important than any technique, or electronic media, or model. What matters is that Granny loved us enough to teach this class. Granny was ninety years old. I went on to other classes, and moved on to teenage things. Granny lived to be over one hundred, and her influence would probably go no further than Bowman, Georgia, which in the 1950 census had a population of seven hundred and forty.

Think about this though: Now I am telling folk all over about Granny. I've shared the story with the Presbyterians, with ecumenical groups, and with countless United Methodists. And I am but one of the little girls in that class. (Ms. Ray Roberts, Media Specialist, East Ohio Conference)

For other adults, it is a reminder of not so good times sitting in a chair, quietly listening to a teacher go on and on about a topic that was foreign to them at the time. Many of them heard about the faith every week. They may have even learned lots of facts about the Bible, the church, Jesus, and Christianity. What was missing was experiencing the faith. They didn't find God's love and presence in their Sunday school experience. For those adults, the name Sunday school conjures up visions of what they remember as a wasted, boring hour every week.

Is it time to do away with the name? This has been done in some churches. Many of those churches have chosen to preserve the experience while renaming it so that the historical stigma is no longer related to their Sunday morning discipling process. Other churches have not only done away with the name, but the experience also. These churches have either given up on Sunday morning educational experiences altogether, or have replaced them with other structures for learning.

Busy Lives

What is life like for the people in your congregation? Many people in numerous communities are working more hours to meet the responsibilities that were spread over several people in the past. One result of companies tightening their belts has meant that those who were able to keep their jobs are required to do the work of more people. This trend has also meant that displaced workers are working longer hours to make the money they need to maintain their lifestyle, or just to make the ends meet. It has required other workers in search of new positions to commute to work—some to the other side of town, some to the other side of the country.

Given these trends in our communities, families have less time to be a family. Add in a few extra curricular activities for members of the family – baseball, scouts, dance, women's and men's organizations—and there just isn't much time left for resting and recharging. Some families have made the decision to let Sunday become that time. Maybe they have become "one-hour" families and attend worship only. Maybe they have decided to take Sunday mornings off altogether and worship at an alternate time, or not at all. The need to rest, rejuvenate, and catch up on chores around the house has wiped out the idea of Sunday as Sabbath for many in our communities.

That's not all the conflict either—there are the sports teams! There has been an explosion of involvement in school, recreational, and competitive teams in the last twenty years. Because of this, communities are no longer able to meet the need for recreational and sports facilities. As cash-strapped communities were trying to come to terms with this dilemma, someone realized that there was a wide-open time block that could be utilized: Sunday morning. Today, in many of those communities, a number of games and activities are going on at the same time as our Sunday school and worship services.

This trend is extending to other parts of our culture. A time of the week that was once reserved for church and rest is being consumed by the business of life, just like every other part of our week. Those who have remained faithful to Sunday school and worship on Sunday mornings have been required to make intentional decisions to honor that time. Their "yes" to church activities has required that they answer "no" to other options.

Leading the Way

Leadership has been a hallmark of strong Sunday schools from the very beginning. It is to those who have responded to the task of faithful teaching and leading as a part of God's call upon their life that we owe the legacy of this organization. Because of dedicated leadership, the Sunday school has changed, adapted, and developed as needed over the years. It will be because of the same dedication of people, gifted and called to this ministry, that the Sunday school will respond to the current need for adaptation and emerge as a vital part of the overall ministry of the church.

Identifying, calling, and training leaders for the Sunday school has become a challenge of crisis proportions. Sunday schools having enough teachers and leaders are rare. There are many reasons and excuses:

"I've done my time. Let someone else take responsibility."

"I've just got too much to do."

"I don't know enough about the Bible to teach."

"I don't want to leave my class. We just have such a great fellowship and I learn so much."

"I have to work some Sundays."

"My family spends some of our weekends at the ___ (beach, slopes, football stadium, cabin, etc.)."

"I'm just too tired by Sunday."

Now, if we really trust God, and believe what Paul wrote about the body of Christ, we have to believe that we have everyone we need to do the ministry we are called to as the church. That means there are leaders and teachers for every need related to the Sunday school. In later chapters, we will be addressing this challenge and all of the others as we look at ways to blaze a new path into the future of the Sunday school.

Numbers Count

There are special challenges in every size church. Lack of numbers, as well as overflowing classrooms, creates special challenges for the Sunday school.

Let's look at the small church first. How do you have a Sunday school program when you have no children or youth? There are many churches that find themselves with one or two children, or none at all. In these congregations, Sunday school may be a viable option for adults, but there is a yearning to be a part of growing something more. Churches in this situation look for ways to engage children beyond their membership in meaningful interaction. Others seek ways to do the "one room" Sunday school effectively. This extends to the Sunday morning experience the concept of the one-room school, which was so long a way of life in our developing nation. In this model, participants of all ages engage in learning together. Meeting the needs of each age group involved can be a challenging task. There are also tremendous possibilities for engaging members of various generational groups together in Christian learning.

The large church faces numerous challenges also. Securing enough teachers for a multitude of classes for children, youth, and adults can become a full time job. Finding space for each of those classes can also become a challenge. Some growing churches use every room possible including offices, kitchens, and hallways. Providing meaningful learning environments in temporary spaces becomes another full time job.

Purchasing curriculum in sufficient quantity and finding meaningful resources for each class tests the expertise of those whose responsibility it is. Some churches struggle to make denominational curriculum designed for a dozen youth work for fifty, while others are either oblivious to the need or overwhelmed by the tasks of adapting independent curriculum to the theology of their environment.

Dealing with multiple services and Sunday school hours becomes another organizational trial for those in larger churches. This challenge becomes an amalgamation of all the earlier ones listed for the large church. How do you secure enough teachers and leaders for Sunday school to function effectively when ushers, choir members, greeters, and many others are needed for the worship services going on at the same time? How do you help teens, who grew up going to Sunday school while their parents attended worship, realize that both worship and education are important elements of a balanced experience?

Churches in-between these extremes face many of the challenges from both ends of the spectrum. Depending on where the church is in relation to growth, funding, and facilities, it could have any of the dilemmas mentioned above, along with some that are unique to their situations. These churches can be in a position of needing a dedicated staff person for ministry leadership, but not being able to afford or secure one. They may need more classes for an age group, and no place to put them. They may have a large building that is no longer needed to maintain their present ministry levels.

Churches of every size have special challenges. Meeting the needs of all is difficult without a plan that is based on foundational elements that translate into every size congregation. Models for ministry are not always easily translated from one situation to another. However, if we have a solid foundation, we are able to build the structure for a Sunday school that works in our church.

Generational Changes

According to Barna Research (http://www.barna.org/FlexPage .aspx?Page=Topic&TopicID=9), each succeeding generation has lower attendance levels in church overall with the exception of the "mosaics" (1984-2002), who are probably more prevalent because they come with their Boomer (1946-1964) parents, and are a larger group in sheer numbers. Overall, lower church attendance levels most likely translate to lower Sunday school rates also. We know that, historically, the young adult population is the most absent group from the church. Providing meaningful ministry that allows people to grow throughout their lifespan will be necessary if we are to turn the tide of this trend.

Curriculum that Works

Even as our denominational publishing houses work to provide curriculum resources that are accessible, theologically sound,
and designed to take advantage of the most recent developments in
research about how we learn and develop as individuals, we are
inundated with independent publishers seeking to fill the per-
ceived voids we find in the denominational offerings. In addition,
there is the desire to develop localized curriculum that specifically
meets the needs of our particular congregation. Stitching together a
number of different approaches to curriculum can be overwhelming to the volunteer teacher, and can tax the professional training
of a staff person. It can also lead to gaps in the learning process for
participants in any given class.

An overall plan for curriculum development and use in the
Sunday school will result in a more comprehensive approach to
Christian education and spiritual formation for class members.
This is true in every age group where we minister. If we know where
we have been and where we are headed, we can more effectively
develop life-long disciples. There is a saying: "If you don't know
where you're going, any place you end up is fine." This is probably
not a productive way to approach Sunday school, or much of anything in our lives!

The Bigger Challenge

While we have looked at some of the specific challenges facing
the Sunday school today and into the future, there are broad-rang-
ing trends that have and will play a part in the path for the future,
if there is to be a viable organization called the Sunday school.

There has been an evolution over the past fifty years that translated into a whole new way of "doing" church and faith
development, especially Christian education. The societal con-
structs that provided the luxury of Sunday school teachers who
were able to devote hours to their lesson, searching out just the

right illustration, craft, and activity, has given way to time-crunched individuals. Today's teachers juggle their Sunday morning responsibilities with job, family, individual fulfillment, easy travel, second homes, and a list that goes on into oblivion! In a time when home schooling is popular and often Christian based, is there really a need for the Sunday school to teach the basics of faith? In many churches today, the sermon is seen as the teaching activity of Sunday morning, with other educational and growth experiences happening in small groups throughout the week.

What impact does the Internet have on traditional Sunday school? Does it become a resource, or a hindrance? In a time when chat rooms, message boards, and blogs populate the world of our children and some adults, how do we encourage human interaction as a vital element of spiritual development? Is the theological perspective of the church valuable beyond the unfiltered proliferation of pop theology and personal views to be found online? As in all of life, this pervasive new technology has come with a price tag, one that allows us to forego community and determine our understandings and definitions based on unseen, novel approaches. It also provides at the fingertips of teachers and leaders a vast amount of knowledge, useful for developing meaningful interactive experiences for our students. This new medium will affect our Sunday school of the future.

Other forms of technology provide other challenges and possibilities. Computers, cell phones, CDs, DVDs, MP3s, PDAs, camcorders, digital cameras, WiFi, satellite, and technologies emerging even as this is being written will have an impact on the experience of the Sunday school.

The Biggest Challenge

The challenges mentioned in the prior section, and others that have not been named here, provide stepping stones and stumbling blocks for us on our way to establishing a more effective setting for Sunday morning Christian education. They might be addressed by working to do what we already do more effectively. Have you ever heard this definition of insanity?

"Insanity: doing the same thing over and over again and expecting different results.

The biggest challenge is whether we are ready to give up that which is most comfortable, and instead rely on God rather than our history. Will we step out in faith, knowing that there is the possibility for reviving this huge giant we call the Sunday school? For most of us, this goes against our nature. It is a call to breech the boundaries between what we've always done and what we can do. It is placing our lives, our ministry, and our very being in the palm of God's hand and saying, "Not my will, but yours."

In this subjection of our will to God's, will we find a new path, one that begins with Jacob, John, and Robert Raikes? This path connects with Granny Bowen and Josephine Spence. It is a path that enables our gifts to be used in the service of our Lord, as we discover new ways to connect our learners with the age-old story.

Thoughts Along the Path

Consider where you are in this time of transition. Use the questions below to guide your thinking about the challenges facing the Sunday school and what that means for you as a teacher and leader in this central ministry of the church.

Which challenge did you resonate with the most?

Do you see other challenges that were not addressed in this chapter?

Do you have any thoughts on where you believe the path of the Sunday school is leading for the future?

3

Classroom Style

Mark and Robert are together for Sunday school. They were at a birthday party together last night. Mark's parents are out of town for the weekend, so he spent the night with his good friend Robert. The boys are great friends, and they do almost everything together, so it is not unusual at all for them to be at Sunday school together at each other's churches. Thus, this morning, they find themselves in the fifth grade class at First Church downtown where Robert's family is very active.

Robert's parents dropped the boys off at the door of their class, and head upstairs to their class. Afterwards, they may or may not stay for the 11:00 worship service, depending on what Robert's parents decide. They have some yard work they have been trying to get done. It's a nice day, so they may head out after Sunday school, get

a quick bite to eat, and then return home for an afternoon of catch-
ing up on their current yard project.

When Robert and Mark enter the room, Mrs. Flannigan greets
them. Mrs. Flannigan teaches the class with her husband when he's
in town. Today, he must be out of town because there's another
lady there that neither of the boys has ever seen before. She comes
over and introduces herself as Mrs. Ingle, whose daughter Jenny is
in the class. After a few minutes of just hanging out waiting for
everyone to get to the room, Mrs. Flannigan asks students to take
their seats in the semi-circle of chairs at the front of the room. Once
everyone is there (about twelve fifth graders), Mrs. Flannigan introduces Mrs. Ingle and calls roll. The offering basket is passed, and
Mrs. Flannigan begins the class.

What happens after the introduction of the lesson? How would
you fill in the lesson plan for the rest of the morning? Does this
opening time seem familiar to you?

The description of the happenings at Robert's church is probably fairly typical of many children's Sunday school classes across
our country. Most often, it continues with a lesson, an activity, and
a worship and prayer time at the end. The elements probably are
tied together through the curriculum used by the teacher. If Mrs.
Flannigan has been teaching for a while, she may be comfortable
looking at the outline for the session in the curriculum and deciding to make some changes. She may have an idea on the same topic
and decide to substitute that idea for a section of the suggested
plan. She may be uncomfortable with the new activity that is suggested and rely instead on one she has used before because she
knows how to do it and she remembers her class liking it.

The second teacher (there should always be a second teacher in
the room) seems new and may not be as experienced. It might be
challenging for Mrs. Ingle to consider stepping outside the bounds of
the curriculum plan and doing something on her own. She might be
likely to follow everything in the book, with no variation. This might
be a good thing. Sometimes, seasoned teachers are so interested in
using their own ideas that they knowingly or unknowingly discount
the ones in the book and miss great possibilities for their classes.

Here are some thoughts from a veteran curriculum developer:

"We provide options and expect teachers to adapt the materials. No one classroom is like any other. The teacher knows his or her students and is free to use the resources as resources. The teacher is the bridge between the plan (what we want to teach) and the students. The resources are there to help."

(Crys Zinkiewicz, Senior Editor, Youth Resources, United Methodist Publishing House.)

Down the hall in the youth department of Robert's church there's a different experience happening:

The high school teacher has just finished playing a pop song suggested for discussion by one of the members of the class. They are now looking at what the message of the song communicates and how it relates to their world and to their faith.

The leader, Steve, is a very personable man in his forties. He has been working on the lesson throughout the week, and has been talking to students in his class and neighborhood about possibilities for the discussion.

"I'd like to hear from several of you about what you think this song is trying to say," said Steve as soon as the song was over.

"I don't really know what it's talking about. I just listen to it because I like the music," was the immediate response from Cameron, a high school freshman.

"I think it's about the struggle of trying to find out who you are instead of just trying to be who everyone wants you to be." That response came from Rose, an eleventh grader who tends to be more on the serious side.

After several more responses from the group, Steve asks everyone to get a Bible. Because of his discussions earlier in the week, and because he knows his students fairly well, Steve has chosen several passages of scripture for the group to look at that relate to the topic of the song. One by one, the group reads the passages, and Steve asks for ideas about how each passage relates to the message of the song. His goal is for the group to understand scripture as a resource for relating to the world of the teens in his class. Throughout all of this, his co-teacher is fairly quiet. Next week, she will lead a totally different style class that begins with Bible study and then uses different activities to help the students understand themselves as called into the world. Her lesson will also seek to connect scripture with the "real world," but it begins in a different place than her teaching partner's lessons.

In this example, the world and the Bible have become the curriculum. Participants in the class are involved in both the selection of topic and the discussion during the class. In the example, Steve has begun with the world where his students live and moved to the world of faith as it is represented in the Bible. On the alternate week, while we do not know what the co-teacher uses as curriculum, we can assume she also seeks a response from participants. Maybe the class participates in a service, mission, or social justice project as a result of the Biblical imperative to be involved in our world. This method begins with the Bible and allows it to speak to the way we live in our world.

Both of these methods are valid and valuable. Both methods also are developed without the benefit of any written curriculum. This leads to some special challenges.

The theology represented is derived from the training and experience of the leader. This can provide a wealth of knowledge and depth. It is also possible that this can provide a dearth of real spiritual strength. The leader needs to be familiar with the theology of the church and how the church wants that theology expressed in the classroom. Leaders in this type of teaching situation also need to be growing in their faith. They should have a clear understanding of who God is for them, and how they arrived at that view.

Consistency depends upon leadership. It is up to the leader to provide this sense of stability for his or her students. What happens when one or both of the leaders for this class are not present? Most likely, someone else comes and "does their own thing" for that week. Having a curriculum plan allows that plan to become one of the consistent elements for the class.

The teachers co-lead, in a sense, but in reality it is more about taking turns. There is not a real sense of team teaching in this style of class. There may or may not be communication between the teachers outside of the classroom.

Upstairs at First Church, Robert's parents are involved in a lively debate in their class about the merits of home schooling vs. public schooling.

Celia, Robert's mom, has some definite ideas. "I don't see how anyone can believe that it is better for children to stay home for school rather than being a part of the bigger world. Robert's school has offered him learning opportunities that home schooling would never be able to offer him."

"Celia, I can understand that, but we feel that home schooling has also offered Luke possibilities not afforded in public schools. We have a time every day for Bible study, we are able to determine his schedule, and we can join other families with the same moral and spiritual base for field trips and activities," this comment coming from Kirk, the father of another elementary age child.

"I can see the advantages, but is that what God is calling us to do?" asked Celia. "Should we insulate our children from the world, or should we teach them to learn to live in a world that has different values than we hold because of our faith? It seems as if we and they have more chances to have an impact on the world that way, and I think that's what Jesus told us to do."

Kirk was ready with a response. "The danger is that the reverse is true. The world has more possibility of having an impact on children. By home schooling, we are able to prepare our children for when they have to interact with people whose values are different."

This class, at least this session, obviously is devoted to how participants raise their children as faithful followers of Christ in a world that is not always supportive of what that means. We have not been able to hear enough to know if this is a discussion over coffee before the real class begins, if we are being treated to a portion of debate central to the lesson, or if this is a discussion class where the topic unfolds and members and a facilitator seek to bring some Christian understanding to the evolving topic.

There are some assumptions we can make about the class, however. It seems clear that Kirk and Celia know each other; they have probably both been in the class for a while. Since the topic of parenting is central to the discussion, it is likely that this is a class of parents, probably of children of about the same age. These parents want their class to speak to the specific needs that they are experiencing now. They need to know how their faith addresses the concerns of parenting.

Adult classes seem to thrive when several elements are present, including:

People have or want to establish relationships with others in the class.

The class is formed around a topic or an approach that is important to participants.

Leadership is established and works to provide meaningful experiences for those who are involved.

Respect that allows differences of opinion with openness that provides the basis for possible growth in the individuals present.

Where We Are

We have taken a quick look inside Sunday school at First Church. We've seen several different styles of classes, and reviewed several different understandings of what should be happening in Sunday school. It is likely that there are a number of different possible responses to what was happening. Let's listen in on some of those:

From Robert's fifth grade class:

"Mrs. Flannigan is so nice; I wish she could be my Sunday school teacher until I graduate from high school."

"That class is so boring. All we ever do is hear a story, play a game, and do some stupid craft. I can't wait until I get into the Youth class next year!"

"The hug that Mrs. Flannigan gives me every week is the best! It just feels like God is giving me a hug. It doesn't even matter what we do. I'd go every week just to get one of those great hugs."

From the high school class:

"All we ever do in there is listen to music or study the Bible. The same people say the same things every week. Do I have to go?"

"Steve is cool. I like the way he lets us decide on the songs we listen to and how he doesn't really plan a lesson. We just talk."

"No one has ever even said 'Hi' to me. I hate going there and sitting for an hour every week. No one at that church even knows that I exist!"

And upstairs in the hallway outside the adult classes after Sunday school:

"I just wish we had a more structured lesson. It seems like we're just exchanging the little bit that each of us knows with each other. Maybe we need a real teacher!"

"Maybe we should switch teachers. We never really get to discuss anything. The teacher has her plan, and she is going to do what she has planned no matter what comes up in discussion."

"I'm so glad that I get to be a part of my class. It is the place where I know I can go with any problem and get help, whether it's prayer or a meal when I'm sick. The fellowship in this group is just great!"

There are as many different ideas about what a good Sunday school should be as there are people in Sunday school—that's millions of people—making it hard to provide a model or a process that will work in every situation. All of our situations are different. This can make it easier for us to just leave it alone for fear of making it worse and think, "So what if we have a few less people in Sunday school than we did last year?" Others of us are ready to do away with it and find a whole new structure for educational ministry on Sunday mornings, as well as other times. There is evidence that these groups are growing, but not at the same rate that Sunday school is declining. At the same time, there are thriving Sunday schools that are growing and changing lives.

Thoughts Along the Path

Take some time to think about Sunday school in your church. What is going on in children, youth, and adult Sunday school in your church?

What do you hear others say about your Sunday school ministry?

What is your own experience?

What is the best way for a person to grow in their faith in your church?

Is Sunday school a part of that growth plan? Why or why not?

4

Building on Shared Strengths

It was an unusual gathering, this group of a half dozen people from various churches and situations in the area. The groundwork was laid for the meeting over a period of time, but this was the first face-to-face meeting.

Over the past six months, each of the people here, and several who were not able to attend, had been corresponding via e-mail about the dilemmas of Sunday school in their particular churches. They were all in different situations, but there was a common thread of wanting to see more happen with and through the Sunday school. Finally, after a flurry of e-mails, a meeting time was set and the group gathered to begin a new journey together.

Linda French, full-time Christian educator at the suburban church hosting this first gathering, called the meeting to order. She had asked Jim Cantrell, Sunday school superintendent from Faith Chapel, to prepare a devotion.

"I thought I'd start off with lettin' you folks know why I'm involved in Sunday school—maybe even the church:

"You see, when I was in seventh grade, I had this Sunday school teacher, Mr. Ed Bennett. I don't really know if he was a good teacher or not. As a matter of fact, if you asked me to tell you about any one lesson he taught in the junior high boys' class (the boys and girls were separated in those days), I don't really think I could tell you. What I do know is that Mr. Bennett liked me. That's saying a lot about an adult, that he liked a seventh grade boy! He called me every Saturday night to let me know that he was going to be teaching the next day (he taught the class every Sunday I can remember), and that he was counting on me being there. I thought I was special. I was impressed that he took the time to make that phone call every week. I wanted to be in class because I didn't want to let Mr. Bennett down.

"I never thought about it until later, but he probably called every boy in that class. He always had a class full of us, and I imagine it was because he called each of us and told us he was counting on our being there. Whether I knew it or not, I learned a lot from Mr. Bennett, and as much as anything else, I learned that it's important to make people feel special.

"I've been trying to do that at Faith Chapel for years. For the past fifteen years, I've been the Sunday school superintendent, and I call my teachers every Saturday night to let them know I'm looking forward to seeing them in their classrooms the next morning. They seem to like the calls, although I leave more messages than I get live people these days. I'm here because I believe God has given us Sunday school as a way to make a difference in the lives of a lot of folks. I just want to see more parents and children take advantage of it.

"The Bible says that we should 'Train children in the right way, and when old, they will not stray' (Proverbs 22:6). I believe it's true, and if we need to do it a different way, I'm glad to know how. I just want to do all I can for our children."

After Jim closed his devotion with a prayer, Linda asked people at the meeting to introduce themselves, tell a little about their church, and give a reason that they were interested in being a part of this gathering. One by one, people told about their specific experiences. They talked about what was working and what their concerns were. They each suggested that they had come to this meeting in hopes of doing a better job with Sunday school leadership in their ministry setting. While every church was different, they all had in common the belief that Sunday school was important and it had the potential to do more than it was doing.

Linda thanked each person as they shared with the group, and at the conclusion of the introductions and sharing, she proposed a process for the remainder of their meeting time.

"It has been helpful to put faces with names, and hearing about our particular Sunday schools just reinforces for me the need for us to join forces to find ways to strengthen all of our Sunday schools. As I have read about the development of Sunday school, I found something that we have in common with leaders over the years. During the two hundred and twenty-five years that Sunday school has been in existence, it seems that it was strongest when it was an ecumenical movement, unifying people from all the denominations to provide a place for education and spiritual growth. I hope we can model that same kind of development. Since we have limited time, and I know all of us want to honor the commitment we made, here, is my suggestion for how we go forward today.

"Let's look at what each of us sees as the strengths of our particular faith community. I think we will find that those strengths match up with growing edges for others in the room or in the community. If that hunch is true, we can become resources for each other. I think we all have the possibility of learning a thing or two along the way."

Linda's church, St. Andrews had a unique way of finding, training, empowering, and supporting their teachers. She put this on the list as a way her church could contribute, and added that they could learn from Jim's weekly phone calls.

Sue Munsey, a schoolteacher and the lead teacher for her Sunday school, was from an outlying church of seventy people. They usually had about forty people in Sunday school, which was an intergenerational affair that met in the church social hall. She felt that her church could offer help for involving people of all ages learning together.

Craig Watson was the pastor of First Church downtown, and was at the meeting because the Sunday school in his church was failing. It had been the flagship church in the area for many years, but in the past twenty years, as people moved out from downtown, there were fewer and fewer members who were willing to come downtown for a two hour experience. They would drive in for 11:00 worship, and then head back to their suburban Sunday afternoon activities. Craig was struggling with what he had to offer the group. He did have a gift for administration. His small Sunday school was well run, so this was an area that it was decided Craig could provide strength for others. Jim Cantrell from Faith Chapel felt that he had gifts to offer in the same area, so he and Craig decided they could work together to help the other churches in administrative leadership.

As people offered what they could, Rachel Hughes wondered what her contribution might be. She had volunteered this year to be a part of a church plant team. The plant, Agape Fellowship, had not yet started meeting, but would begin its life in a local school. They would use classrooms for Sunday school and the cafeteria for worship. Rachel's husband, Marc, was the pastor, and her role was to work with children and youth ministries. The work so far had focused on developing leadership. To that end, Marc, Rachel, and the rest of the team had been leading discipleship training in homes for anyone who felt called to leadership in this new venture. They had also spent a great deal of time seeking God's guidance and responding with strategic planning for their ministry. As she shared this with the rest of the group, they asked her to consider spiritual discernment for overall direction as what she could offer.

The remaining participant was Elizabeth Matthews. She was a Sunday school teacher for second graders at Bethel Bible Church on the edge of town. She had been teaching since she was a teenager, and her teaching defined her life. Elizabeth had seen many of her children grow up, graduate, get married, and have children that were then a part of her class. She struggled with how many teachers came and went, and the lack of stability she felt was foundational for children as they grew up in the church. She wanted to offer her ideas on caring leadership.

"Well," said Linda, "It looks as if we have several specific areas that we can concentrate on for what we can offer each other. I suggest we all go back to our churches, invite some other people from our congregations to join us, and get to work on refining the areas we are going to share. Let's set another meeting date, and at that point plan to present some basics from each of the areas of strength we have identified. Does Saturday morning work well for all of us?" All heads nodded in the affirmative. "Okay, I suggest we meet on the ninth of next month. That should give us all time to get some work done. Anyone want to close our meeting with prayer?"

Rachel volunteered:

"Dear God, as we spend time in the next few weeks looking at what we have been able to accomplish with your help, enable us to see beyond the work that we are doing, to the good that we can bring about, as we seek to more effectively minister to your children through the Sunday school. Bless each of us in our work and in our walk. We pray all of this in the name of your son Jesus, our teacher. Amen."

With that, words of thankfulness were exchanged with new friends. Everyone looked forward to a new beginning aimed at making Sunday school in area churches a more meaningful experience.

Thoughts Along the Path

Often, we can see our faults easily. They are so glaring that we are not as cognizant of our strengths. Looking in this direction first can empower us to build on that which we already do well, enabling us to grow through the challenges that face us.

Identify two strengths of your current Sunday school ministry.

Identify two churches in your area that would benefit from your strength shared with them.

Name two churches that could share their strengths with you and your congregation, allowing you to grow in the effectiveness of your Sunday school.

If you are struggling to identify other churches, perhaps another option would be to make plans to meet with someone in educational ministry of two other churches in your area in the next month.

5

Collective Planning

The month came and went in a hurry. Anticipation was in the air as the group assembled for its second meeting. Everyone from the original meeting was present, and several had invited others who had joined them to work on their particular topic.

This time the group met at First Church and the pastor, Craig Watson, followed the leadership pattern established at the first meeting as he called this meeting to order.

"As with the first meeting, I decided we should start with a time of devotion. I have asked Sue Munsey to share some thoughts with the group. Sue?"

"Thanks, Craig," said Sue. "I really liked how Jim Cantrell gave us a peek into his life and experience of Sunday school. I decided to ask Angela Halter, who came with me today, to share her experience."

"When Sue asked me to share with you today, I was excited. I wanted to be able to tell you my story in a way that might give hope to some of you who wonder if you make a difference.

"We went to church because it was the proper thing to do. Relationship with God? What was that? Sunday mornings were just one more day out of the week that I had to get up earlier than The Price Is Right. That was until someone changed that for me. I remember walking into the classroom on Promotion Sunday and being overwhelmed by a sense of comfort that seemed to start at the top of my head and pour over me like a pitcher of water. With a smile on my face that reflected the happiness that the room seemed to evoke for all that entered, I couldn't help but soak it all in. There were brightly colored walls decorated with posters that encouraged children to "love one another" and "do unto others as you would have them do unto you." There were loving pictures of Jesus sitting with children, laughing, and even hugging and holding them. All of these things made me feel as though I had truly walked into God's home.

"As I continued to take it all in, I noticed a tree made of paper on the far wall. Part of it was taped to the wall, and the other part created a 3-D effect. I have not forgotten that tree, or the story of a little man that climbed up into one similar to it to see our Lord and Savior Jesus Christ. You see, my teacher brought the Bible to life. She not only told the story, but we experienced it. Her love, compassion, excitement, and commitment to Christ make up the example of the Sunday school teacher I hope to one day be."

"That's why I teach in our intergenerational program, and why I wanted to be a part of what you are trying to accomplish through this project. Maybe together, we can increase the number of children who experience what I got to experience, not just in our church, but in churches throughout our area."

(In real life, Angela Halter is Director of Children and Youth at Platt Springs UMC in South Carolina.)

"Angela, your story reminders me about why we do what we do week after week," Sue said. "I appreciate your sharing. Now I would like us all to join in a prayer to conclude the devotion time.

"Loving God, you are the source of all that we are. As teachers and leaders in the Sunday school, we are reminded by stories of changed lives that the possibilities for making a difference in the lives of children, youth, and adults are many. Inspire our time together, and inform the ministry we are seeking to do together, so that we continue to learn even as we teach, and continue to love with your love in all that we seek to accomplish for you. Amen."

"Angela and Sue, you have set the stage for what I think has the potential to be a great time together. Thanks to both of you," said Craig. "Now, let's talk about what we've accomplished during the past month."

Linda said, "I brought our outline of how St. Andrews identifies potential teachers and leaders, and the process we use to move from identifying them to securing their leadership, training, and involving them as leaders. I'm just wondering what we do with the information now?"

"Craig and I wondered the same thing. We've been working on how to turn Sunday school administration into a caring ministry, but we weren't sure if we should have it all printed up or what," said Jim.

Rachel raised her hand. "I have the process we've been using at Agape Fellowship for vision and direction, but it would really be important for me to be able to tell you about it in a way you could understand it, instead of trying to put it down on paper."

"It sounds like we need a plan on how to go forward so that we get the most from our work," remarked Elizabeth, the Sunday school teacher from Bethel. "My lessons always go better when I have a plan. I do everything I can to make the plan fit the children in my class that particular year. I don't want to miss anything that might help me do a better job with the precious children I teach. Maybe we should look at an organized way to share what we've come up with?"

"I agree," said Linda. "It seems like so much of what we do when we try to fix Sunday school is haphazard. I really want our work together to count for something. Maybe we need to use what we have worked on to provide a series of workshops—not just for ourselves, but for anyone in our community who is looking for ways to make what they do more effective."

Craig chimed in. "That sounds like an excellent plan! I know that what we've accomplished so far would be helpful to those of us who started this process, but why not enlarge our efforts to as many people as possible?"

The group spent the rest of its time deciding on a schedule of workshops for making the Sunday school a more effective organization. Participants planned contact strategies for other churches and assigned responsibilities for each workshop. They decided the group would host one workshop per month on the first Tuesday of each month for the next six months. This provided for time to get the word out, prepare the workshops, and time in-between for people to put into practice what they had learned.

As a part of each workshop, there would be a time for sharing what was working and where churches needed more help. There would also be an implementation packet given out at each workshop on the topic presented. The hope was that with the presentations, packets, and discussion sessions, people would not only have information, but would have all the tools they needed to make Sunday school more effective.

Thoughts Along the Path

What did you think of Linda's comment "...so much of what we do when we try to fix Sunday school is haphazard." How is this true in your situation?

What is happening in Sunday school in other churches in your area? How might you find out?

Think about the value of churches collectively trying to strengthen Sunday school. What affect might that have on your Sunday school?

6

Appreciative Inquiry Toward Vision

It was decided that Rachel would lead the first workshop on the topic of visioning. She and her husband Marc spent a lot of time talking about how the process they had been using for their church plant would work as it was applied to Sunday school. After a lot of thought and prayer, they decided that Appreciative Inquiry would be an effective way to help churches recognize strengths in relation to Sunday school. It would also build on those strengths to move toward a future that could allow more people to take advantage of what Sunday school could offer them.

Marc had discovered Appreciative Inquiry as a part of a conference he attended that focused on organizational development.

It had proven to be extremely helpful as he and his team had moved into a new community and started the process of building a community of faith from the ground up.

Appreciative Inquiry is about the co-evolutionary search for the best in people, their organizations, and the relevant world around them. In its broadest focus, it involves systematic discovery of what gives life to a living system when it is most alive, most effective, and most constructively capable in economic, ecological, and human terms. AI involves, in a central way, the art and practice of asking questions that strengthen a system's capacity to apprehend, anticipate, and heighten positive potential. It centrally involves the mobilization of inquiry through the crafting of the "unconditional positive question" often-involving hundreds or sometimes thousands of people. In AI, the arduous task of intervention gives way to the speed of imagination and innovation. Instead of negation, criticism, and spiraling diagnosis, there is discovery, dream, and design. AI seeks, fundamentally, to build a constructive union between a whole people and the massive entirety of what people talk about as past and present capacities: achievements, assets, unexplored potentials, innovations, strengths, elevated thoughts, opportunities, benchmarks, high point moments, lived values, traditions, strategic competencies, stories, expressions of wisdom, insights into the deeper corporate spirit or soul—and visions of valued and possible futures. Taking all of these together as a gestalt, AI deliberately, in everything it does, seeks to work from accounts of this "positive change core"—and it assumes that every living system has many untapped and rich and inspiring accounts of the positive. Link the energy of this core directly to any change agenda and changes never thought possible are suddenly and democratically mobilized [David L. Cooperrider and Diana Whitney, *Appreciative Inquiry: Collaborating for Change* (San Francisco: Berrett-Koehler Publishers, 1999)].

The whole idea of a life-giving organization was appealing to Marc, who had experienced other forms or organization that he felt limited the potential for God's spirit to lead in the direction a group or church was being called.

After a lot of work, the presentation was ready. The night came, and Rachel stood before a room with about fifty people, representing a dozen different churches from the community.

"I want to welcome each of you to this first workshop on how we can empower the Sunday schools in our churches to become more than they are today. Throughout its history, Sunday school has changed and adapted to the needs of the society where it was located. No longer is it the only place for children to learn to read and write. No longer is it the only study setting in the church. No longer does it avoid conflicts between church and community, conflicts that might steer participants in a different direction during that hour on Sundays. The Sunday school faces new challenges. Even without a lot of hard facts, we can see by what is happening in most of our churches that attendance, which means involvement, is declining.

"However, in case we grow concerned about the possibility of Sunday school disappearing, we need to keep in mind that according to a recent survey by the Barna Group (Sunday School is Changing in Under-the-Radar But Significant Ways, July 11, 2005), there are sixty-seven million children, teens, and adults involved in Sunday school. Of interest as we look to the future of the Sunday school, this same research said that forty-five million of those in Sunday school are adults, and the most likely places to cut Sunday school classes are for preschoolers and junior and senior high school youth. Looking at these trends, we can see that our future population will continue to shrink unless some significant changes are made.

"My presentation tonight can be a beginning for our congregations. I want to share with you a process that can significantly affect the future of the Sunday school in your church. The great thing about this process is that it allows us to end up in the place that is right for our congregation. This is not a model of ministry, it is a process for enabling positive, God-inspired change to happen in and through our local congregations as we respond to the call we are experiencing as communities of faith. I want to invite you to begin our exploration of this process called Appreciative Inquiry.

"Appreciative Inquiry is a way of exploring what gives human systems life when they function at their best. It is a way to discover what the strengths of an organization are, and to build on those strengths to enable the dreams or vision of those involved in the organization. This process works well in the church because it is a relational process. It is based upon the assumption that everyone in an organization has something to give. Sounds a lot like Paul's description of the body of Christ, doesn't it? Could we have someone read the scripture on the screen?

A teenager who was with Sue Muncey's group read aloud:

> For just as the body is one and has many members, and all the members of the body, though many, are one body, so it is with Christ. For in the one Spirit we were all baptized into one body—Jews or Greeks, slaves or free—and we were all made to drink of one Spirit.

> Indeed, the body does not consist of one member but of many. If the foot were to say, "Because I am not a hand, I do not belong to the body", that would not make it any less a part of the body. And if the ear were to say, "Because I am not an eye, I do not belong to the body", that would not make it any less a part of the body. If the whole body were an eye, where would the hearing be? If the whole body were hearing, where would the sense of smell be? But as it is, God arranged the members in the body, each one of them, as he chose. If all were a single member, where would the body be? As it is, there are many members, yet one body (1 Corinthians 12:12-20).

"Also related to this passage is the idea that we are stronger when everyone has a part in who we are becoming, than when only a few decide for all of us. In the church we understand this to mean that God works in and through us. Appreciative Inquiry gives us an effective way to live out this incarnational theology.

"Let's look at the overall process. In the diagram, you can see that there are four parts of Appreciative Inquiry, and that is a circular process. We are always somewhere in this process, and when we work through the process in one arena, it is time to identify a new one for exploration.

"Tonight, our mission is to look at how we can utilize this positive process to move forward to a new future in our local churches' Sunday school.

"Let's begin by looking at the Discovery step. How do you discover 'the best of what is' in your Sunday school? One possibility might be to gather the people who are currently involved in your Sunday school ministry, and ask them to share with the group what they see as best. This is a place where you have the opportunity to share and hear stories. Do we have anyone who would like to share a story with us about their best experience in their Sunday school?

Appreciative Inquiry "4-D" Cycle

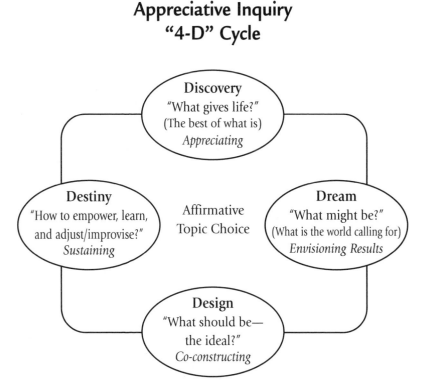

AI 4-D model taken from "AI Training Module" by David Cooperrider, Weatherhead School of Management, Case Western Reserve University, Cleveland, Ohio. 2002. Source: The AI Commons website: http://ai.cwru.edu

"How do you discover 'the best of what is' in your Sunday school?"

Rev. Cathy Williams, a minister on the education staff of one of the larger local churches volunteered to share:

"When I was first getting into Christian education, many years ago, I attended a workshop for Sunday school teachers. There were many brand new teachers, and also some twenty to thirty-year veterans. We were all asked what we each remembered from our own Sunday school experiences. What were our most important memories from the days when we were children going through Sunday school? The answers that came forth were not the ones I expected. I had expected to hear that these dedicated Sunday school teachers had remembered receiving some great theological insight, or some unique interpretation of a Bible story in their Sunday school classes that transformed their lives. Instead, what I heard were stories of how important the relationships were that were experienced in those classes—stories of a teacher who took the time to listen, an adult leader who hugged a student who needed hugging, and cookies and treats that were provided by a Sunday school teacher who cared. Over and over again, from young and old, both the new teachers and the more seasoned, the importance of the relationship they experienced from their own Sunday school teachers was lifted up. That was a lesson to me about what is truly important when we teach the word of God: It is more caught than taught, and it is crucial that we exemplify the love of Jesus in our classrooms with our students."

(In real life, Cathy Williams is a Christian Educator in the Miami area.)

Rachel resumed. "Thanks Cathy, that is an inspirational story. I'm sure if we use this exercise in our own churches, many of us will hear similar stories about people's experience of Sunday school in their lives. While we could spend time talking about those who have had a bad experience in Sunday school, the purpose of Appreciative Inquiry is to learn about, and then build on, the positive that we are already doing. This approach is much more life-affirming than one that is problem-centered. Giving people credit for their life-enhancing involvement with others is a richer way of living out Jesus' mandate to love one another, than seeking to lay blame and create a negative climate while looking for what's wrong in our churches. The Discovery phase is a great place to involve as many people as possible in this process. Helping our congregations be a part of moving into the future will ease the transitions when the time for change arrives.

> "...the purpose of Appreciative Inquiry is to learn about, and then build on, the positive we are already doing."

"Looking at our diagram, you can see that the next phase is the place we get to Dream. As followers of Jesus, our question for this phase is: 'What are we being called to do to meet the needs of our world?' What is the vision for Sunday school that we have in mind as we build on that which we have done well in the past and present?

"I want to give you some time to talk with a partner about your dreams for your Sunday school. At the conclusion of those discussions, write your dream on the large white sheets of paper on the wall. I'll let you know when it's time to move on."

> "What are we being called to do to meet the needs of our world?"

After about fifteen minutes, Rachel encouraged people to begin writing their dream statements on the paper taped to the walls. The dreams reflected some familiar themes. Here is a partial listing of them:

More teachers than we need.

Teachers who are excited about their involvement.

Students who are engaged and excited about growing in their faith.

Students and teachers who are building deep relationships with each other and with God.

Curriculum that is easy to teach with meaningful content reflecting theology that is consistent with our church's understanding of the Christian faith.

Classrooms where creative leaders utilize traditional and innovative approaches to teaching and learning.

Comprehensive teacher and leader formation, teaching skills and forming disciples.

Families who make church a two-hour commitment on Sunday mornings.

A new name that better reflects what Sunday morning Christian education is about.

Around the room, dreams of a transformed Sunday morning experience were emerging. People were wandering around looking at what others had written, and were commenting about how the dreams of others related to their own dreams of building on what has gone before to meet the needs of their current situation. They also discussed the challenges of a new path for the future.

Rachel called the group back together. "It is obvious from the dreams we have listed around the room, and the conversations that are happening throughout the room, that there is excitement about the possibilities for the Sunday school of the future. Maybe it has a different name, and it definitely sounds like there could be new forms, but it is obvious to me that we all see the need to help grow Sunday school into the future. So, let's look together at what we can do with our dreams.

If you choose to use the dream process in your own church, here are some questions to consider:

Who will you involve? Some people to consider would be Sunday school teachers and leaders, your pastor, general church leadership, and Sunday school participants of differing ages.

How will you dream together? This example has used discussion and writing. What other forms of dreaming might be appropriate for your process?

What result are you looking for? Is an image sufficient? Does your situation need something more specific? Is there need for prioritizing?

"Looking again at our chart, we can see that the third phase of Appreciative Inquiry is called Design. In this phase, we look at how our dreams are integrated into our organizations. Ultimately, we are talking about changes in our churches to incorporate our dreams into who we believe God is calling us to be. How will our churches look when our dreams are in place? How will our Sunday schools be organized? Taught? Resourced?

> Ultimately, we are talking about changes in our churches to incorporate our dreams into who we believe God is calling us to be.

"These are questions we can't answer here. They are questions that will need to be worked through by a broad spectrum of people in our local churches. Maybe they include the same people who were a part of the dream phase. Maybe there are others who need to be included because they have expertise in particular areas such as education, theology, organizational development, curriculum, or spiritual discernment. Utilizing your strengths to build for your future is the key concept here.

Who are the people in your congregation who should be included in the design process? Which leaders and participants in your Sunday school, church, and community do you need present to allow you to discern the path for your future?

"The outcome that is necessary in this phase is called the Provocative Proposition. You may emerge from the design phase with one or several propositions, depending on the dreams that you are striving to integrate into your present structure for Sunday school. These Provocative Propositions may determine a different way of structuring the Sunday school in your church, or they may call for a more extensive change in the way your entire church operates. The purpose of any organization is to accomplish the goals of those who have come together to form the organization. If the Sunday school is integral to the overall goals of your church (and it should be, or you shouldn't have a Sunday school), then changes in your Sunday school organization may also require complementary changes in your overall church structure.

> The purpose of any organization is to accomplish the goals of those who have come together to form the organization.

"The responsibility of the design group would be to fashion a Provocative Proposition about how that will be lived out in your congregation. The statement will be presented as if the future is now, thus painting a present form of the future reality. The statement reflects the present strengths of your congregation that we discussed in the Discovery phase. The statement is provocative; it challenges your church to reach beyond where it currently is. As we read scripture, we are continually reminded of the call to have faith. We are to believe more than we can see, to be more than we understand how to be. The design phase meets us where we are on the journey and paints a picture of who we are to become as we discover a new path.

An example of the Provocative Proposition process:

You have proposed, "More teachers than we need" as your dream for your Sunday school. Your Provocative Proposition might be: "Our Sunday school ministry has at least two teachers as the teaching team in every class, with an ongoing invitation and training program providing sufficient leadership for each new Sunday school year."

"The final phase of the Appreciative Inquiry process is the Destiny phase. In this phase, everything from earlier phases comes together. As a church, you will want to work on plans and a process to accomplish the dream that has been stated in your Provocative Proposition(s). You will want to recognize changes that have already happened as you have worked through the Appreciative Inquiry process. You will want to examine your structure and determine whether you have the leadership already organized to accomplish what you are setting out to accomplish. If not, you will need to create a new structure that will better serve your Sunday school of the future.

"Let's look at each of these tasks.

"Many times, we as the church come up with wonderful goals for our congregation. We work to refine mission and vision statements. We envision new futures that would help us change our world. The challenge is to move these grand ideas from paper to reality. This is where we are challenged to put our money where our mouth is! This is where the hard work begins. Determining how you as a congregation will move from having a good idea to having an improved ministry is the strategy phase of this process. Who will do the work? How will it get done? How will it be funded? How will we know when we get there? What is the timeline for moving from where we are to where God is calling us in our Provocative Proposition(s)? All of these are questions for the Destiny phase. This phase is about a plan and a process to move from where you are to where you believe God is calling you as a congregation.

"Just as people got excited here tonight as we began to name our dreams for Sunday school in our churches, excitement will build in your congregation as you work on this process together. Some changes will begin to happen as participants in the process go about their responsibilities of teaching and providing leadership in other ways in Sunday school. This is a natural experience, and it needs to be celebrated. You need a way to gauge change that occurs throughout this transition time, and you need an avenue to celebrate the change that happens. Sometimes, this process is like spontaneous combustion. People have been waiting for something new, and when the concept is introduced, the results begin to manifest themselves. Be ready, recognize, and acknowledge this progress.

"One of the areas the church has strength is in our organization. Every denomination has a structure for accomplishing ministry, and every church has adapted to a structured way of doing what they do. Even my church, which is a brand new, non-denominational church, already has organizational structure emerging. It is our nature to develop structure that will organize our corporate lives. An important question related to the use of Appreciative Inquiry in our churches is whether the current organizational structure is adequate for accomplishing our dreams. In the case of the Sunday school, do we have the right people and the right processes already in place? Perhaps there is a need for new insight. Perhaps the skills we need to reach the place where we are living our Provocative Proposition(s) in our organization are different than the current makeup of our education committee. Maybe we could benefit from cross-pollination with other areas of leadership in our church. Perhaps we can organize events like the one we are doing here, and derive new insight from those outside our current situation.

Prepare for the Destiny phase by asking the following questions:

Who is the leadership body for Sunday school currently?

Do they possess the necessary creative outlook to move us from where we are to where we want to be?

Who is present in our congregation (groups or individuals) who could add to our ability to reach our dream?

Are there others in the community/church structures beyond the local church who could be helpful?

"As a congregation, your biggest challenge is to move from having painted a future that you believe is your calling as a congregation, to living into that future. The Destiny phase is about that process."

Rachel gave participants a minute to let that last statement settle in. She knew from her own experience that this phase was the most challenging, but also that it was the pay-off. It is where you actually see tangible results that your world is changing for the better.

"That is a summary of the Appreciative Inquiry process as we might apply it to the Sunday school. As you will note if you refer back to our diagram, it is also the final phase. As you near the completion of this phase, you should be looking forward to new areas of your ministry that you can build on for the future. AI is a continuing process that has the potential to change the way we do what we do in the church in a positive way. It provides a framework for our efforts to see the vision God has projected for us, and respond as our unique communities of faith have the potential.

"This concludes our first community Sunday school workshop. Remember to put the first Tuesday of next month on your calendar for our second session. Also, feel free to invite others to join us. Our goal is to share information that might be helpful to churches with as many people as possible."

Thoughts Along the Path

For many, Appreciative Inquiry is a new process. Here are some questions to consider as you ponder the potential of it as a guide for your congregation's discovery of God's vision for Sunday school.

How would I introduce this process?

What do I hope to accomplish by using AI in my congregation?

Who are the people in my congregation that would be able to grasp the concept of AI and interpret it to others?

Am I prepared for the change that could happen if we used AI to map a new path for Sunday school?

7

Naming the Purpose

The group decided that the next workshop would be called Leading the Sunday School. Craig Watson from First Church, and Jim Cantrell from Faith Chapel, were the facilitators because of their experience in providing overall leadership for their respective Sunday schools. Jim had served as the Sunday school superintendent for the past fifteen years. Craig had served as the pastor at First Church for almost as long.

The aim of the workshop was to help participants recognize overall leadership of Sunday school as an opportunity for ministry, rather than just a necessary task. Craig and Jim met every week for the month preceding the workshop to design a session they thought reflected how the whole organization of a Sunday school in a church community could reflect this concept of care.

Craig began. "My name is Craig Watson, and I am the Pastor of First Church. I have worked throughout my ministry with the Sunday school, because I believe it is an essential part of making disciples in the church. Jim Cantrell, who will be co-leading tonight's session, is the Sunday school Superintendent at Faith Chapel. We want to welcome you to tonight's workshop. Our focus tonight will be on providing leadership for Sunday school in your faith community in a way that reflects the care that we see exhibited in the early church when they came together for fellowship, study, and worship. Jim will begin our time together by reading from Acts 2:42-47."

They devoted themselves to the apostles' teaching and fellowship, to the breaking of bread and the prayers.

Awe came upon everyone, because many wonders and signs were being done by the apostles. All who believed were together and had all things in common; they would sell their possessions and goods and distribute the proceeds to all, as any had need. Day by day, as they spent much time together in the temple, they broke bread at home and ate their food with glad and generous hearts, praising God and having the goodwill of all the people. And day by day the Lord added to their number those who were being saved.

Jim continued after he finished reading the scripture. "As you can see from Acts, teaching and prayer have been a part of what it means to gather as followers of Christ from the very beginning. We don't want to underestimate the importance of food, either!"

"I know that many of you are Sunday school teachers. I was a teacher in our Sunday school for years before I became the Sunday school superintendent. How many of you folks have served as teachers at one time or another?" Every person, about forty, raised his or her hand.

"Since each of you has been a teacher," Jim continued, "you know how important it is to have a support system for your teaching.

You can teach every Sunday of your life and not accomplish what you want to accomplish without some basic systems that allow you to focus on your class and its particular needs.

"Those systems are what we want to talk about tonight. Now, if you are a part of a small church, you may think you really don't need much in the way of organization for Sunday school leadership. But even the smallest Sunday school can benefit from knowing who is there, what you're trying to accomplish overall, and how you're going to do what you set out to do. Craig is going to start with something so basic, we don't even usually talk about it in the church."

"Thanks for that introduction, Jim," Craig said as he moved to the front of the group. "We want to begin with a look at the purpose of the Sunday school. We've chosen to have one of Jim's church members share her experience of Sunday school with you. We want you to listen for the purpose that has been served by Sunday school in her story. You may want to take notes so we can discuss what we've heard together afterwards."

Jim walked forward, accompanied by an older woman whom he introduced as Ali Turner.

Ali smiled at the group and began. " I am happy that Jim has asked me to share with you tonight. Sunday school has been an important part of my life, and I would like to share with you about a time when it was the key element in my very survival.

"I arrived here early in the new millennium, after spending a lifetime in my beloved Kentucky. Bruised and achy from a recent divorce, I made the move to restart my life living near two precious grown daughters. I was also adjusting to my life as a retiree, having just celebrated the end of my thirty-year career in high school guidance counseling. I felt as if I were a lost ball in high weeds. The transition did not look to be easy.

"As I began to settle in and started looking for a place to worship, I wandered with trepidation one Sunday morning to a yet another new church. My approach to the worship service took me on a long courtyard path lined with what appeared to be entrenched parishioners, most of whom paid me little regard.

'Could I ever fit in here?' was my immediate question. Fortunately, the message from the pulpit that day warmed my heart and brought me back for return visits.

"One Sunday, a friendly man graciously greeted me in the pew where I sat. When I inquired about Sunday school, he invited me to attend an adult class called The Forum. The very next Sunday, my journey in faith took a completely new turn. I became a member of that Sunday school class.

"This class consisted of devout Christians seemingly determined to enhance their discipleship through intense scriptural and theological studies. The format of the class was given to book studies with thoughtful discussion centered on the application of Bible teachings in today's world. I was introduced to Christian writers who opened to me new faith vistas and enabled me to more readily feel God's Holy Spirit.

"We tackled some of the most controversial subjects facing today's church, society, and our own families. All topics were viewed under a microscope, so to speak, as they related to scripture. Never before had I been involved in a study where argument and debate took place in such an atmosphere of love and acceptance. No question or idea seemed inappropriate, and erudite exchanges resulted in transformations toward deeper awareness and more dedicated discipleship.

"I felt so blessed to be in this place with God clearly in our midst. God was moving and altering lives. God spoke to me personally! God created for me a new depth of perception, and yes, even offered up a few dreams and visions and demolished a wall or two. My Sunday school 'fellows in faith' as I called them, became a most important part of my life. My new friends were people who really practiced the church's mission to make God's love real.

"God was only beginning to touch me! About a year after my introduction in Sunday school, I was diagnosed with leukemia. The prognosis was poor. My mind raced. Could I tolerate treatment? Could I be healed? Could I go to heaven? What is heaven? Could I just live to see a new grandchild yet to be born? How would I pay for the recommended treatment? Why the fear, when I was a child of God? Could miracles still happen? I spent many sleepless nights tearfully trying to hold strongly to my faith, while praying nonstop.

"During the next several months, I prepared for a stem cell transplant and the long period of recuperation. My Sunday school class continued in a valued life support role. They listened when I needed to talk. They shared in my joy over the news that my only sibling, a brother, had just tested to be a perfect match as my stem cell donor. This was an exciting result, as the chances of a sibling match are only one in four. Next came home visits with gifts of food and lots of encouragement. Then there were prayer vigils, phone calls, cards, and letters.

"I traveled to Seattle, Washington for the clinical trial treatment of my rare form of leukemia. Forum Class members followed with generous donations to a trust fund to help with the expense of my prolonged stay in a hospital and clinic there.

"The treatment and recovery were brutal. However, I consistently felt the reassuring hand of God. I felt the comfort of the Spirit. During one long night while in intensive care, I had a vision of Jesus sitting in a chair by my bed. I attribute these experiences to the loving, Christ-like influence of my Sunday school class. It was there, with those Christians, that my faith was strengthened. It was there that I came to know with certainty the unconditional and everlasting love of my Savior. God worked through this committed group of people—Christ's flock. I listened for God through each member and heard God over and over.

"Long, trying months after my diagnosis, I returned to my still new home as a leukemia patient with the results of my last bone marrow test still ringing in my ears: "Cancer free!" My class continues to support me in all things, as they do many other people. I have overcome many fears, one of which was being inadequate in serving God. Fortunately, through the love, witness, and nudging of my Forum Class friends, I have found several ways in which I, too, can make God's love real to others. Thanks, Forum Class, for bringing God's kingdom to my doorstep and into my heart."

(Ali Davenport Turner is in real life a member of the Forum Class at Hyde Park UMC in Tampa, Florida where she lived out the story shared here.)

"Thank you, Ali, for sharing your inspirational story," said Craig. "Now, let's spend a few minutes talking about the purpose of the Sunday school in light of what we heard from Ali. Take a few minutes with two or three people around you and compare what you wrote down during Ali's sharing."

There was quite a buzz as people started comparing notes on what the purpose of the Sunday school was. Ali's story had given several aspects of what the Sunday school can be, and people were talking about the purpose they heard in her story and the purpose they see for their own church. After about ten minutes, Jim called the group back together.

"Let's see what we came up with in our discussion time. Craig will record what we are sharing as we let each other know about what we discovered as the purpose of Sunday school." The groups shared from their discussions, and the list Craig was making began to take shape. Here are some of the items listed in the smaller groups:

- To provide people a smaller community within the church where people can belong.
- To provide meaningful teaching and learning experiences for participants.
- To provide a safe place for persons to struggle with their beliefs.
- To enable people of all ages to learn about being in relationship with Jesus.
- To study the Bible.
- To understand what it means to be a Christian.
- To provide support for members who have specific needs and challenges.
- To empower participants to discover untapped potential.
- To train leaders.

People went on to list a number of other purposes of Sunday school. These reflected both their current state of affairs, as well as their hopes and dreams.

"Obviously, we have a number of different ways of understanding the Sunday school and it's purpose," said Craig as he referred to the list in the front of the room. "Holding this type of discussion in your own church would yield responses that more closely reflect the thinking of your own membership. I encourage you to write down what we have named here, however, because you may find that something on this list may strike a nerve with others in your circumstance.

"We can't know where we are going if we have no roadmap. Just doing Sunday school every week because we've done Sunday school every week is not taking us in any direction. Actually, as we look, we may discover that we are accomplishing some elements of purpose very well, but we may miss the opportunities we have to improve and invite more people to be a part of what we are doing. If you were here for the last workshop, you will remember that the Appreciative Inquiry process can help us be deliberate about discovering how we are doing and how we can build upon our strengths to be more effective."

What is the purpose of the Sunday school in your church?

How many of your teachers and leaders have a working understanding of the purpose?

Who would you gather to determine the purpose of Sunday school in your setting?

Is there someone in your church whose story would capture the purpose of the Sunday school like Ali's story did here?

Jim spoke next. "Once we know what we are about as the Sunday school, we need to understand how we can best organize to accomplish our purpose. Most of us have been doing Sunday school the same way for years and years. Maybe the way we do it is the best way possible for us, but it may be worth a look at what we do and why we do it that way. Maybe we can learn something from each other that will help us do a better job in our own church. I want you to get with the people from your church and use one of the sheets of paper on the back table to describe how you are organized for Sunday school. Include how you divide your classes, how many teachers you have for the number of students in your classes, and anything else that you think is important about how you do Sunday school."

People from eight different churches were present, so they gathered in groups around the room to accomplish their task. Even in their groups, participants were learning new information about what was supposed to be happening at their church, and trying to reconcile that with reality. At the end of fifteen minutes, Craig asked each church group to join another church group and share their descriptions with each other.

As groups began sharing, they discovered that there were a variety of ways that churches in their areas organized for their Sunday school ministry. Most had a traditional schedule meeting for Sunday school before the weekly worship time on Sunday mornings for about an hour. Some had Sunday school assemblies where everyone joined together first for announcements, singing, and prayer, but most separated by age groups as soon as people walked into the door.

One church had a different way of organizing for Sunday school. Sue Munsey and others from her church shared about how they do intergenerational Sunday school after worship. They share their minister with several other churches, so worship has to be earlier. This has facilitated their Sunday school ending with a covered dish lunch once a month.

Linda French and the contingent from her church talked about the challenges of multiple worship services and having Sunday school at the same time as worship. The numbers of people involved vary from hour to hour, and so the way they organize Sunday school for children and youth at different hours must be adjusted. At one hour, there are classes for every age level. At the other hour, there is one youth class and one children's class, much like the smaller church they were paired with.

Craig called the groups back together into a total group, "What have you learned?" he asked.

"I learned how things were supposed to be organized at our church," said one participant.

"I learned the importance of clear communication between teachers and leaders," chimed in the Sunday school superintendent from the same church.

"I realized that we have never really looked at why we do what we do the way we do it."

Another person added, "I'm looking forward to getting the leaders of my church together to look at the purpose of Sunday school and decide if the way we are organized right now is the best way to accomplish that purpose. I really like how Sue's church begins with worship and ends with Sunday school, rather than the way we've always done it. I think that provides potential for some great ways to encourage fellowship."

"I really like the idea of teaching teams. I've been the second grade teacher at my church for seven years, and always feel guilty when I can't be there. I find a substitute, but the children don't always know them. If I had a co-teacher, I would feel better about not being there, and they could share some of the planning and teaching all the time!" said an older gentleman in the group.

"I was surprised to hear how many different groupings for teaching are happening right here in our community. There is everything from churches that have a class for every age group, to Sue's church where everyone is together. I know that there must be challenges with each one, and I'm curious to learn more. Maybe we need to look at changing how we group people for Sunday school."

"It looks like we've stirred up a lot of interest as we've shared what is happening in our churches," said Craig. "That's just what we wanted to accomplish. We'll look at some of the areas mentioned here tonight, and more of them in future workshops. More than anything else, we wanted you to see that there are many ways to do what we do. The real lesson is that your way of organizing for ministry should be in direct response to the purpose you are trying to accomplish. Every church should be intentional about understanding the purpose of their Sunday school and planning everything they do to serve that purpose."

You may want to meet with the leadership of your church (not just Sunday school leadership) and spend some time looking at how you are organized for Sunday school. Ask the group to consider the following question:

"Are we organized for the best possible outcome in Sunday school, given our purpose?"

"Okay. There are several items we want to cover before we end our time together tonight," Craig continued. "The first is related to the teaching teams mentioned earlier. There are great reasons for having teachers work in teams, and two were mentioned earlier: it provides coverage when one teacher is out, and it allows for the planning and leading to be shared. Another reason is safety.

"While we should know all of those who teach in our churches, it is important that we have teachers working in at least pairs. A screening process should be in place for all of our volunteers who work with children under the age of eighteen. This provides an extra measure of safety for everyone involved in our Sunday school ministry."

"You're right," said a man from the back row. "Recently, a man who was arrested for abuse was a leader in his church. I don't want to judge people, but I do want us to do everything we can to protect our kids."

"That is exactly why we suggest a process for all of your volunteers. If you check with your denominational leaders, they should be able to give you some guidance on putting a child protection policy into place. Your church liability insurance carrier should also be able to give you names of companies or agencies that do background checks for your volunteers. One resource that I know about because we've used it is called *Safe Sanctuaries, Reducing the Risk of*

Child Abuse in the Church [Joy Melton, (Nashville: Discipleship Resources, 1993)]. There is also a version for youth called Safe Sanctuaries, Reducing the Risk of Abuse in Youth Ministries."

Jim said, "We also want to spend a few minutes talking about an element of Sunday school that I have focused on in my church. What I'm referring to is caring for teachers. We ask teachers to be a caring presence in the lives of the students in their class, but we also need to find ways to care for our teachers. It may be that the satisfaction of sharing their faith through teaching is enough to keep teachers motivated, but I have a hunch teachers need more. Because of this, I work hard to help teachers know that I care and try to find small ways to let them know how important their leadership is.

"Every Saturday night, I call each of my teachers just to let them know that I'm looking forward to being in ministry with them the next morning. Sometimes I talk to them, and lots of times I just leave a message. When I do get to talk with them I try to find out what's going on in their lives. I promise to pray for each of them, and I do! On Sunday mornings, I make it around to every room before things get started and greet each teacher by name. I ask if there is anything they need, and if I can, I get it for them."

"I teach at Jim's church," said a woman on the second row. "Knowing that Jim cares enough to stay in touch, and that what is going on in my life is important to him, sure gives me some added motivation for continuing to teach. It makes me want to be there every Sunday, too."

"Thanks, Jeannie. Everyone needs to be a part of something that meets his or her needs. This includes our teachers. I also inquire in our conversations about how each teacher's faith life is going. You can't always be giving; you need a place where you are connected to God as your source, too. If our teachers are growing, I figure our students will be also."

How do you care for your teachers and leaders?

"Now, you thought you were going to be hearing all about taking attendance tonight I bet," Jim continued. "I hope you have caught a glimpse of where we are going with ways of organizing for Sunday school that are life-giving. Attendance is important. It's how we know who we are in ministry with and who we need to be reaching out to. What I hope you've discovered tonight is that those kinds of functions grow out of what we are trying to do—how we live out our purpose. When what we do is firmly planted in the Source of Life that motivates us, all of the other will fall into place.

"Thanks for being with us tonight, we'll look forward to seeing you at the next session. Invite as many Sunday school teachers as you can. The next couple of workshops are especially for them."

Thoughts Along the Path

Does your church have a child protection policy? Here's how you can start:

1) Contact your regional denominational office for guidance.

2) Contact your church liability insurance carrier for advice on the policy and for resources to do background checks.

3) Find a workbook like Safe Sanctuaries and use it to implement a program for all adults working with children and youth eighteen and younger.

8

Gifted to Teach, Gifted to Thrive

The third workshop in the series had a dual focus: 1) helping people respond to God's call to teach, and 2) helping them find ways to be spiritually nourished as teachers. Linda French from St. Andrews Church was the leader for this session. Her church had worked over the past several years to approach the need for a sufficient number of teachers in a more holistic way. Their Sunday school was large, and begging to get someone in every classroom was not satisfying the need for teachers, nor did it feel appropriate for a community who believed that God would supply their need for teachers, just as they believed that God would supply their needs in every other area of ministry. Linda was excited to share what her church had learned.

"Welcome to the third of our workshops on Sunday school. As you probably know, these workshops came about because of the need felt by representatives of several churches in our area to increase the effectiveness of our Sunday schools. The two earlier workshops have been more general in nature. Tonight is more specific. It's great to see so many of you here. So let's get started."

Addressing the seventy-five people present, Linda began. "We could not have Sunday school without teachers. They are the cornerstone of the Sunday school. We can have a class meet just about anywhere. We can divide groups in many ways, so that we have sufficient students to form a class. We can find curriculum that gives us step-by-step instructions on what to do. All of these help create a Sunday school class, but the teacher is the key. The teacher is the one who makes curriculum come alive. The teacher is the one who can knit individuals in a class into a bonded family. A teacher can meet almost anywhere and still accomplish the goals for a class. As I said, the teacher is the key.

"If we look back to the life of Jesus, we can see what I've been talking about. He certainly didn't have ideal conditions for holding class, and had no control over who or how many people would be in his class. Still, he was able to teach because it was what he was called to do. Jesus was living out his destiny as he shared insights with those around him that enabled them to grasp the message of God's love. Jesus empowered them to live as new creations. Just as Jesus called his disciples to serve God, so we are called to serve today.

"Teaching is not about filling slots and finding enough warm bodies. It is about discovering whom God has planted among you with the gift to teach, and empowering that gift to allow it to thrive. In his workbook *Teaching Today's Teachers to Teach* (Abingdon Press, 2003. p. 27), Donald Griggs says, 'Usually when we go begging, we get a beggar's response; we receive a pittance of a person's interest, energy, or commitment.' Instead, God has called us to find those who are gifted and encourage them to release that gift in ministry among us. It is a very different way of going about finding teachers for our Sunday school.

"How many of you are here because someone told you they needed you because they couldn't find anyone else?" Over half of the room raised their hands. "You are examples of how we need to change. You were probably also told it wouldn't take that much time and everything you needed was in the curriculum." Heads were nodding throughout the room.

"The good news is God is a God of grace, and we have not been left hanging. God is always with us and supplies the needs we have to do the ministry we need to do. The better news is that God has given each of our communities the resources we need to fulfill our roll in sharing the Good News. Among us are the teachers we need to do what we are being called to do in the Sunday school. I've asked Christian Faux from my church to talk about his experience of teaching at St. Andrews."

"Linda, thanks for the opportunity to be here. As Linda said, I am a teacher at St. Andrews. My wife and I moved here not long after we got married because the company I worked for transferred me. We really missed home, and a big part of what we missed was our church. We both grew up in the youth ministry there, and knew everyone. It really was our second home. When we moved here, the first thing on our list after finding a place to live was to find a church. St. Andrews is a lot like the church we both grew up in, so we joined after visiting it and a couple of other churches.

"Not long after we joined, we met the Education Director. He was the person who held that position before Linda. We were looking for a young married class to get involved in. He told us they didn't really have a class for people our age, but they really needed teachers for the junior high class. Because of our age and our involvement in church growing up, he thought we would be perfect.

"I have to tell you that neither one of us really wanted to teach junior highs, but he kept pushing. We were looking for a place to belong, so we finally said yes. He handed us a book, told us where the room was, and said he would check on us next week. We took the book home and tried to figure out how to do what it said we should do. It did give step-by-step directions, and after several hours, we had a plan. It wasn't quite as easy to plan as the Education Director said it would be, but we just figured it was because we were new at this. We were ready; or at least we thought we were!

"The next Sunday rolled around, and we were in the room ten minutes early. There were already two guys in the room horsing around (no wonder their parents got them there early!). We introduced ourselves and told them we were the new teachers. Their response floored us: 'Do you think you'll last longer than the three that came before you? Most of them didn't come back after the first time.' Well, that was information we didn't have, and now we wondered what we had gotten ourselves into. As kids came in, we introduced ourselves and tried to remember their names. Then we started on the curriculum. Immediately, one of the early boys said, 'I can't believe you're going to use that stuff, we've heard everything in it about a hundred times!' I didn't remember Sunday school being like this when I was in junior high. I thought you were supposed to respect adults just because they were adults.

"By the time the hour was over, I wanted us to join the parade of teachers who had come and gone before us. But as my wife could tell you if she were here, I'm a little stubborn. I decided that I wouldn't let this group of disrespectful junior highs get the best of me. I went home and worked on a battle plan for the next week. We finished the year teaching that class. I wish I could tell you that everything got better and we ended up having a great experience, but it really wasn't like that. When we were done, we decided that was the last of teaching for us. We went to worship and left every Sunday, still missing what we were looking for when we got roped into teaching the junior highs. We really wanted a class of people who were our age and going through the same things we were. We wanted a place to explore what it meant to be young, married, and Christian. We had begun to talk about finding another church when Linda came to St. Andrews.

"Someone told Linda what we were looking for, and she called us. She asked if we would meet with her to look at the possibilities of forming a new Sunday school class for people in our age group who were married. We couldn't wait! This is what we had been looking for, what we had been praying for! When we met, it was great. Linda had some ideas about other couples in the congregation, and we knew a few of them. She asked us to prayerfully consider becoming the leaders of this new class. After our junior high experience, we weren't so sure. She said she just wanted us to pray about it for a week.

"As my wife and I talked and prayed over the next week, we knew that this was what God had called us to. We felt sure this ministry needed to happen, and that we could help make it happen. When we met with Linda again, we told her we would do it. She said she had suspected that we would, and immediately told us about a workshop on starting new Sunday school classes that was being held by our denomination. I was able to get off work to attend and came back with lots of ideas about how to get started. As we were identifying people for the class and getting organized, Linda heard about a conference on twenty-somethings, and my wife and I attended. The experience inspired us, taught us more about how to understand the needs and interests of our own age group, and gave us tons of ideas for study material for the new class.

"Our class has been meeting for three years, and we are the main teachers. As we prepare to teach, we look forward to how God will use us and our lesson to help us and our friends grow. We now have a family in this town because of this class. People in the class are beginning to have babies, and we are sensing a transition in the class, but I think we'll stay together no matter what. We know that God has called us to be in leadership in this place. It's totally different than our first experience at the church.

"I hope that your teaching is more like our second experience, not our first. Thanks for letting me share it with you."

"Christian, thanks for sharing your experience," Linda said. "Can any of you identify with his experience?"

"With the first one or the second one?" came a jovial response from the crowd as they laughed.

"With either?" continued Linda.

"I think I was the teacher before them in that junior high class!" joked one attendee.

"Well, I've been teaching junior highs at St. Andrews for the last three years, and I love doing it as much as Christian loves what he's doing. We've talked about it, and the difference is that Linda helped me find my calling, gave me training, and let me do what I believe God has called me to do. I think I have the best class in the world!"

"Matt, it seems that you've identified a real key," Linda said. "Teaching is about listening to God's voice and responding. Listening and responding includes several things. I want us to spend the rest of our time tonight looking at how we do that.

How do you secure the leadership you need for teachers in Sunday school?

"Let's look at how we might start transitioning toward a teaching ministry that allows God to work from the very beginning.

"God is at work in our lives and in our world in ways beyond our understanding. Who could imagine some of the occurrences in our lives? And yet, they take place. The unexplainable happens every day. If we open our lives to those possibilities, we will see and experience God's presence, leadership, and support.

"I decided a long time ago that I couldn't believe this in one area of my life and not in another. So, if I am going to trust God about my finances, and if I am going to trust God to meet my needs in other areas of my life, then I have to trust God when it comes to this challenging part of my job. I have to believe that God is able to supply the teachers and leaders we need to do the ministry God is calling us to do. This may seem very simple to you unless you have been the person responsible for staffing Sunday school classes in your church. It's usually the issue closest to us that is the hardest to give over to God's control.

"When I came to St. Andrews, I decided the church and I needed to begin a new way of doing things. I spent a lot of time with my pastor. It was important that he understand how I thought God could work in the lives of those in our congregation to supply the need for teachers in our educational ministry. The message had to come from the pulpit, as well as from me, if we were to be successful. What has happened is nothing short of phenomenal! The idea spread to other areas of the church, and we simply trust that God will actually supply the needs we have. What a novel approach for a church." People in the crowd were smiling because they could identify with the irony of the statement.

"In case you are wondering, I didn't just sit back and wait for people to come through the door of my office saying, 'I think God has called me to teach fourth grade.' But I have relied on God's guidance, and the gift of discernment God gave me, to identify people who seemed to have potential for teaching. Christian and his wife are examples. I called them, but I encouraged them to use the opportunity to seek God's council on what was right for them. Sometimes when I do that, the answer is not what I had hoped for. Sometimes temporary arrangements are made for a class until we find the person God is calling to teach it.

"For the next fifteen minutes, I would like you to move your chairs around so you are circled with those from your church. Talk about how you find teachers and how that compares to the way we've talked about tonight."

What would it take for you to shift from a needs based recruitment of teachers to a "calling" based approach?

Who would need to be involved?

How does this relate to the purpose of your Sunday school?

After the allotted time, Linda called the group back together. "We aren't going to discuss what went on in your groups. This is a topic for discussion with the leadership of your local church. Hopefully, we've started that process tonight.

"Now, we are going to shift gears to discuss something that should be of vital interest to all of the teachers with us tonight. We are going to answer a question together: How do we, as teachers, remember that this ministry we are a part of is about the Source of Life, empowering us for ministry?

"It is so easy to stay busy preparing our lesson for the coming week, calling members of the class who need to hear from us, leading the class, and then starting over the next week. How can we see this as God's ministry, and understand that we are participants also? Well, that's the task before us, so let's get started.

"In her book, *Teaching as a Sacramental Act* Mary Elizabeth Mullino Moore suggests that there are six acts of sacramental teaching:

Expect the Unexpected. This involves believing that God is going to act through you as a teacher in ways that are unexpected and unplanned. Moore says that expecting the unexpected 'has to do with traveling with others on the long journey of faith, expecting surprises along the way.'

Remember the Dismembered. Things happen in our churches that cause pain, hurt, and loss. Much of this is hidden under the surface and resurfaces in unhealthy ways. Recognizing hurtful and painful situations, and allowing healing to take place, is important. Providing care for persons in these times can help them remain a part of the church and the faith, even as they struggle to find new life.

Seek Reversals. This act is related to 2 Corinthians 5:17 where Paul says, 'Therefore, if anyone is in Christ, he is a new creation; the old has gone, the new has come!' Moore says we can expect that God will act in ways that are different than we expect God to act. She suggests God's action can be a 'bold reversal in the status quo...Christians can expect the tradition to offer as many questions as answers and to upset comfortable beliefs, values, and social structures...

Give Thanks. Giving thanks is an act of wonder before God.' Giving thanks, as an act of sacramental teaching, can take many forms: We give thanks for the opportunity to teach and the possibilities that it presents; we thank God for each student and the blessing that they can be and become; we are thankful for the grace that allows us to be in a place spiritually to be a teacher, and the grace that can permeate the classroom and lives as the teaching and learning process unfolds.

Nourish New Life. The sacramental role of teachers is to nourish seeds of new life wherever they are found.' What Moore is really saying here is that we are all farmers. Ours is the opportunity to plant seeds, water them, feed them, and trust God to enable growth into flourishing plants.

Reconstruct Community and Repair the World. Sometimes the promise of transformation calls a congregation to fan sparks of life from their dying embers; sometimes, a congregation is called to die and be reconstituted; and sometimes congregations are led into ministries quite different from those they have practiced in the past…[sacramental teaching] has also to do with mediating God's prophetic call in the church and the world.' In other words, in Moore's last act of sacramental teaching, we are called to be a catalyst for change where change is needed. Teaching can be prophetic as well as nourishing and supportive. We know the struggles of the prophets in the Old Testament. God may also be calling us experience struggles so that needed transformation can take place [*Teaching as a Sacramental Act*, Mary Elizabeth Mullino Moore (Cleveland: Pilgrims Press, 2004) pp. 30-37].

"Now, I would like you to turn to the person next to you and discuss what you think about Moore's concept of 'sacramental teaching.'"

The room erupted with animated conversation as the teachers gathered for the workshop discussed this idea. For many, it was different from the mechanical, practical training they had received, assuming they had any training at all. Linda gave the group about fifteen minutes to complete their discussions, and called them back together.

What kind of training have you experienced for the teaching that you do?

What kind of training does your church or denomination offer?

How could the concept of "sacramental teaching" be incorporated into your training?

What difference could this make for teachers in your Sunday school ministry?

"Let's take several minutes to process what we've heard and the discussion time you had with each other. Any comments?"

"It all makes sense, but it's also really foreign to anything I've ever heard before. All of my training has been about how to teach the lesson, take attendance, and relate to the age group in my class." This comment came from a woman in the middle of the group. There were a number of people nodding their heads in agreement.

"I find this idea of sacramental teaching intriguing, but also a bit frightening! I thought I was supposed to teach a lesson and keep the teens in my class interested. Now I hear I'm supposed to be changing the world!" This from a young man named Scott, whom Linda had met at one of the earlier workshops.

"Remember what Gandhi said, 'You must be the change you wish to see in the world.' This way of looking at teaching is really about putting yourself in God's hands, and allowing change to happen in and through you," was Linda's response. "It is different to think of ourselves as 'world changers,' rather than just someone who prepares a lesson for Sunday school each week.

"Let's look at how that transition might take place for you and your teaching.

"First, where are you receiving your spiritual nourishment? Do you attend worship each week? Some teachers find that preparing to teach—actually leading their class, having after-class discussions with participants and parents, and clean-up time at the end—makes it difficult for them to get to worship on time, if at all. While it seems like that makes sense, it also means that you are missing out on an essential element of your spiritual growth. We can only continue to give if we are also being replenished. If Sunday morning doesn't work for you, I encourage you to find an alternate time when you can experience worship. Your witness in this area is also vital for the students in your class. Worship and education are both essential to a healthy spiritual development, so your leadership can be life changing for those whom you teach.

"Second, what are you doing to put yourself in God's path? Where in your life are you allowing time and space for God to work? It is so easy for us to fill our lives that we sometimes miss the possibilities for God's spirit to act in us, so we continue to grow into the people God is calling us to be. We can even do this as we try to be 'good' Christians.

"I am reminded of a woman I knew who was involved in a Bible study somewhere in our community almost every day of the week. She taught children's Sunday school and was a youth leader in her church. Some of the classes she took were about how to be a Godly woman, wife, and mother. The funny thing is, she was so busy going to her Bible studies, doing her homework, preparing for Sunday school and youth group, she had very little time for her family. If we are to become a vehicle for God's spirit to act in and through the people we teach each week, we must allow God to work in us. The first step in this is to open our lives to the possibility of God's work in us.

"I want to give you some time to talk again with your partner about ways you open yourself to God. Take about fifteen minutes and then let's report in."

Again the room came alive with conversation. This topic seemed to have hit a chord with those present. Hearing snippets of conversations, Linda was sure that the reporting time would be fruitful. At the end of the allotted time, she asked for responses from the participants.

"First of all, this is taking some getting used to. I signed up to teach because it was my turn. Everybody in my adult class takes a turn, and it's mine again. I haven't really ever thought about teaching as a gift, or a sacrament, or part of my own spiritual development.

I've always seen it as my duty. As my partner Jill and I have been talking though, I see where my participation in my class when I'm not teaching is part of how God prepares me for when I do teach."

Linda commented, "That's a great observation. It is also a reminder to all of us who teach that we need to also be in situations where we are the student. Maybe we rotate so we can be in a class as well as teach? Maybe we find other groups and studies to join at a different time during the week? The point is we all need that nourishment of being a student."

A teenage girl named Katie, who was here for the first time, spoke up next. "I am a teen aide and help with a children's class at my church. Since I can't go to my own class, I am a part of a program called Disciple Bible Study. The group meets every Wednesday night and is systematically going through the whole Bible. That is where I am getting to be the student. The group also is a support group for me, and we have time for prayer each week. I can't wait for Wednesdays. They are the highlight of my week!"

"Richard Foster's *Celebration of Discipline* has been a guiding force in my spiritual journey," stated an older gentleman in the group. "My class studied it years ago, and I've worked to practice the disciplines as a regular part of my life since. My favorite quote in the book is from the first page of the first chapter: 'The desperate need today is not for a greater number of intelligent people, or gifted people, but for deep people'" [*Celebration of Discipline*, Richard Foster (San Francisco: Harper 1988) p.1].

"Thanks for that resource. Foster's work on inward disciplines, outward disciplines, and corporate disciplines gives us an excellent framework for structuring our spiritual lives," Linda added. "For those of you familiar with the Wesleyan tradition, you may be able to relate to John Wesley's works of piety and works of mercy. Together, they make up what he called the means of grace. Foster and Wesley provide useful ways to enrich our spiritual lives.

Foster's Disciplines

Inward Disciplines
Mediation
Prayer
Fasting
Study
Outward Disciplines
Simplicity
Solitude
Submission
Service
Corporate Disciplines
Confession
Worship
Guidance
Celebration

Wesley's Means of Grace

Works of Piety
Public Prayer
Family Prayer
Praying in our closet
Receiving the supper of our Lord
Searching the scriptures by reading hearing, meditating
Using such measures as fasting and abstenience as our bodily health allows

Works of Mercy
Feeding the hungry
Clothing the naked
Entertaining the stranger
Visiting those that are in prison, or sick, or variously aflicted
Instructing the ignorant
Waken the sinner
Quicken the lukewarm
Conform the wavering
Succour the tempted
Contribute in any manner saving souls from death
(*The Sermon on the Mount,* Vol.2 p.166, John Wesley)

"At the heart of this session is the concept that, while teaching may be what we do, being a teacher and responding to God's call in our lives is a different matter altogether. I hope that you have discovered some insights in this session that will enhance your journey as a follower of Christ, as well as your journey as a teacher.

"Our workshop next month will focus on the caring ministry of a teacher. I hope you'll be able to be a part of it."

Thoughts Along the Path

How are you finding ways to grow as a follower of Jesus?

How does teaching mesh with your faith?

What spiritual disciplines do you practice on a regualr basis?

Identify one area of your life where you think growth would be important.

9

Care Giving

When the time came for the workshop on caring through teaching, Elizabeth Matthews was ready. For years, she had worked hard to let her students know that she loved them and cared about what was happening in their lives. She had watched them leave her class and go on to other classes, where the teachers seemed to just be trying to make it through the hour then packed up and left until next week. It seemed that the students in their classes were just names on the roll sheet, not real live people with needs and concerns. Elizabeth saw this as her opportunity to make a difference for her students and students in churches throughout the area.

It was January, and the weather had been bad. Elizabeth noticed the tires on her car slipping several times as she drove to the church for her workshop. She wondered if the attendance would be lower tonight. She was disappointed because she felt that what she was addressing was so important. But she really did believe that God would have present those who should be there, so she busied herself getting ready for her session. Throughout the room, she set the chairs in groups of three or four. She had also asked Craig, Jim, Linda, and Rachel to personally greet everyone coming in the door. She wanted the atmosphere to reflect the topic of caring.

Just as she finished arranging chairs, some of the others from the planning team arrived. Elizabeth gave them instructions and directed them to the doors to greet people as they arrived. It was good to see the number of people who were turning out. Maybe Elizabeth's concerns over the weather were not warranted after all. The set-up was working. As participants found seats, others joined them. The way the chairs were grouped encouraged conversation to happen naturally. The room was almost full when it was time to begin.

"Good evening. My name is Elizabeth Matthews, and I will be leading the workshop tonight. Our topic for the evening is the caring ministry of teachers. In our last session, we looked at teaching as an extension of who we are as followers of Jesus. Tonight, we want to look at caring as a natural outgrowth of who we are. It's not really about doing certain things, although we will talk about some specific ways we can communicate care. It really is how we go about doing everything we do in our teaching ministry. If we do it right, not only are we caregivers in our Sunday school classes, but we provide avenues for our class members to become caregivers for one another. I've asked a friend from church to share her amazing story about how God provided for her through the caring of her Sunday school class."

Connie Funk moved to the front of the room to address the group. "I'm sure that as you look at me, you see a young, energetic, healthy, woman, and what you see is who I am today. If you had known me two years ago, you would have seen something very different. After a routine checkup, I was referred to a nephrologist and diagnosed with focal segmental glomerulosclerosis. Quite a name, isn't it? What it really meant to me was that my kidneys were failing.

It was hard to believe at first. I made the dietary changes that the doctor ordered, and still felt really good. As time went on though, I started feeling nauseous and needed more and more down time. My husband and I had always wanted a family, and because of the disease, we decided to adopt. Eighteen months after our adoption, I could hardly move. I had no energy at all. My kidneys were giving out, and I was afraid I was going to die and leave my wonderful husband and the baby we had wanted for so long. I began dialysis when our son turned two. It was the kind you self-administer at home every night for nine hours, and the pain was the worst I had ever experienced. I lost twenty pounds and was vomiting all the time. I knew that I had to go forward with a transplant if I wanted to have any kind of quality of life. The problem was that the wait for a kidney was at least a year and a half, and I didn't have that much time. Several members of my family offered to give me one of their kidneys, but the doctors were afraid that the disease would perpetuate itself in the similar tissue.

"So, we made a prayer request in our Sunday school class. We asked members of the class to pray for me to receive a kidney soon. To our amazement, God answered our prayers immediately! On Monday after we had requested prayer, our phone started ringing. Four men from the class offered to give me a kidney! We were amazed at how God was working in these people who have been a part of our lives for as long as we've been a part of St. Luke's. After eight hours of testing and twenty-five vials of blood, the doctors decided the man who was the best match for me was a member of our class named Chris. He said that all his life he had been taught to think of others first, and this seemed like something he could do for someone else without too much detriment to himself. The operations took place, and I have a new life because of the overflowing love from our Sunday school class."

(In real life, Connie Funk lives in Houston with her husband Scott and their two children. Chris is a frequent visitor to their home and is known as "Uncle Chris" to their children. They attend Sunday school at St. Luke's United Methodist Church in Houston. The Funks would want

you to know that organ donation is an important way of caring for oth-ers in your Sunday school class, church, and community.)

"Thanks, Connie. Your story is a remarkable testimony to how God's love can provide caring ministry through the community of the Sunday school. Her story is a great example of what we heard as the reason most adults go to Sunday school. The top reason is for the relational aspect of being a part of a class. It is because adults find a caring community that loves them and supports them through the tough times, as well as being there to celebrate with them in the good times.

"Your chairs are arranged in groups of threes and fours tonight. I'd like you to take some time in those groups to list ways that car-ing happens in your Sunday school. There are sheets of paper and markers for your lists in the back of the room. We'll use your ideas as a basis for the rest of our discussion tonight."

The groups jumped in, as they had on previous occasions, to discuss the topic of how caring happens in their Sunday schools. Some of the groups were from one church, while others were a mix-ture of people from various churches. Elizabeth wandered through the room, listening for cues about how the groups were doing. Here is some of what she overheard as she ambled about, weaving in and out of the groups:

"I'm not sure why we're talking about this. I thought I was going to come here and learn how to be a better teacher."

"Well, it seems to me that this is one way that we can become better teachers, sharing Christ's love in all we do."

"We have someone in charge of caring in each of our Sunday school classes. That way I can concentrate on the lesson."

"I call the children from my class who miss a Sunday, when I have time. It's just so hard to add that to everything else I am doing each week."

"The youth in my class are great about being a caring commu-nity, if the person in need is one of their group. I just worry about the youth who have a hard time fitting in. Should I be the one car-ing for them?"

"My class is so large, and they are so active, I do well to even get the attendance sheet filled out. I don't even know who is there most of the time."

"We added a second teacher because of the session I came to last month. It has allowed us to do a much better job of following up on people in our class each week. One of us can concentrate on leading the learning activities for the day, and the other can pay more attention to the people in the class. We plan to alternate roles each week. I think we'll be in a much better place in our caring ministry soon."

After her journey through the room, Elizabeth returned to the front. If the comments were any indication, there should be some lively discussion when the group comes back together, and it was about that time.

"Take about three more minutes to record your thoughts on the paper you have," Elizabeth announced, "and be ready to share them with the whole group."

Groups scrambled for supplies, and soon they seemed to have completed their lists and were waiting for further instruction.

"I'd like each group to have a representative come to the front of the room and add the items on your list to the large sheets taped to the wall. If someone has already put an item on the list, just add a mark beside it so we can know how frequently it was listed. This is a good time for the rest of us to take a quick break. We'll come back together to review what we've listed in about five minutes."

The list was shaping up:

- Calling people when they miss class
- Send flowers and cards when something significant happens
- Call new people who visit our class
- Greet each child when they enter the room (by name as much as possible)
- Prayer time at the end of class
- Ask youth to include new teens
- Make sure my responses are as caring as possible

Try to include everyone in class discussion/activities

Have new people fill out information cards/sheets

"This is a good list. It would be wonderful if we were all doing everything on this list. I'm sure all of us do some of these when we have time and remember, and some of us do some of these all the time. I want to suggest that there are some categories that can help us do a more organized job of caring. Even as I say that though, I want to ask you to remember that caring is not just about specific things we do. It is about the reason we do the things we do—to share God's love with the children, teens, and adults in our classes. You're probably going to wonder why I've included some of these. Hopefully I'll explain them so they make sense, but feel free to ask questions if you have any.

How does caring happen in your Sunday school?

"The first category is about our relationship with the people in our class. Each item can apply to you or to your teaching team, if that is the structure you use."

Know Your Students

"In days gone by, teachers actually went to see new students in their homes. This isn't very practical anymore. Today, people might think it odd to have someone come to visit from Sunday school. It is important, however to get to know your class members. Any ideas how you might do this?"

"I do call new members during the week after they come to my class. I have some fairly standard questions I ask that allow me to get to know them to some degree," said an adult Sunday school teacher.

"I try to visit with new teens after class. Sometimes I get to meet their parents, but a lot of times they come with friends or go outside to meet the rest of the family," said one of the youth teachers in the group.

A children's teacher from the same small group chimed in. "I guess I have an advantage. Parents must check their children in before they go to their class or to worship at my church, so I get to meet them when they arrive with their child. My teaching partner and I rotate greeting the children and involving them in activities as they arrive. That way we both get to meet parents."

"Those are great ideas," said Elizabeth. "They are great ways to begin a relationship. Just remember that relationships develop over time."

Use What You Learn

"Now for the second one. Find ways to engage your students in conversation. That probably means being in your classroom early and hanging around at the end. Help your class plan outings and activities that allow for free flowing times of conversation and interaction. I imagine Jesus having great conversations with his followers on their road trips as they walked along, and around the campfires at night. I'm sure that is where they got to know him best, and he was able to share his ministry with them.

"The two we've just talked about are major. Below are some other ways that we can encourage relationship building between leaders and students, and students with each other."

Celebrate, Share, Pray, Involve

"Have a birthday calendar and celebrate upcoming birthdays and special events, like anniversaries, etc.

"Build in the opportunity for sharing joys and concerns as several of you mentioned above. Pray as a group and remember your students in your prayers throughout the week.

"Involve students in ways they can share their gifts and expertise. If you are looking at a time period in the Holy Land, and you have a Middle Eastern history teacher among you, ask him or her to contribute to the lesson. If you want to use music with something you are doing in a youth class, and you have several musicians, invite them to play or sing the music. Ask them to find an MP3 of the song you want to use. Let children provide artwork to illustrate your lesson and share it with parents and others in the church. These are just examples. Your creativity will enable many of your class members to be in ministry with you.

"Share your faith, experiences, and feelings with your class. The more vulnerable you are willing to be, the more open your class members will become. This helps you move from being a class and teacher(s), to being a community and leader(s) growing together.

Category: Developing Relationships
Know your students
Use what you learn
Celebrate special events
Share joys and concerns
Pray together
Involves students
Be vulnerable

"The next category is one that will surprise you. Part of being a caring leader in your class is doing a good job at record keeping. Here are some ways that keeping good records allows you the ability to be a more caring leader."

Know Who Is There

"Being able to put names with faces is important. Remember the television series, Cheers? The theme song talked about a place where everyone knows your name. Well, this is a lot more important in a faith community than it is in a bar! There are several ways of keeping attendance, in addition to sitting everyone down and calling their names. Check people off as they arrive. Greet them and have them sign in and you can check your memory against the name they record. Put a sign-in sheet on the wall and watch as each person signs in, attaching their face to their name. Take turns with a co-leader so that each one of you does the check-in on a regular basis to allow both to learn names. What's important here is learning the names and having a record of attendance. You'll be surprised how quickly your memory fades about who was in class, as your week gets crowded with other tasks.

Know Who Is Not There

"There are two categories here: those who usually attend and are absent, and those who are on a list, either yours or the church rolls, who have never been there. Knowing who is absent can be helpful for several reasons. Any ideas what those reasons might be?"

"They might be sick"

"Or their child might be sick."

"Maybe they're out of town."

"Perhaps they are in a shared custody situation and are with their other parent every other week."

"There might be something going on in the family and they really need support from the church."

"They might be upset about something that happened at church or in your class."

"All of these are good speculations. I'm sure some of you have run into those situations. The point is that knowing who is absent gives us a way to follow up and provide caring ministry in those situations."

Elizabeth was excited that people had recognized so quickly the importance of following up with absentees. "There is an important step here though. Recognizing what might cause someone to miss, and actually knowing why, is separated by a phone call, e-mail, or text message. Being concerned about someone who is missing is important. Acting on that concern is caring."

"What about those names that are on your roll year after year that you never see?"

"We take them off if they don't attend after two months," said a man from one of the larger churches in town.

"We keep them on forever," followed a woman from a smaller church. "If we didn't, even though they never come, you can be sure they would find out about it and then things would get sticky. Everyone in my church is related to about three families. Word spreads fast about everything, so we just keep them on the list."

Elizabeth asks a new question, "What would happen if you began to find ways to care for those people too? What could you do?"

"We could invite them. It might not work, but we could still invite them."

"I think we could pray for them. Maybe we find each of them a prayer partner in the class, and let them know that they are being prayed for?"

"Maybe we could have a special event a couple of times a year and try to really encourage them to be a part of those events. If they liked what they experienced, maybe they would come to our class."

"Again, you have great ideas. With the information you secure through registering attendance, you can better direct your efforts toward those who need to feel your care."

Connect

"The next step in caring through record keeping is to have a way to connect what you know to what others know. You probably only have one or two members of a family in your class. If something is going on in a family, tracking the whole family can help you recognize and respond with God's love. Maybe the pastor needs to be the person responding to a need. Maybe a teen needs an extra nudge because parents have decided that they are old enough to make their own decisions about church involvement. Sharing information can help us all become a more caring community."

Category: Keeping accurate records
Know who is there
Know who is absent
Check on regulars who miss
Invite and encourage others on your list
Connect information throughout the Sunday
school/church

"The next category of care is about interaction in the classroom session. Our acceptance and respect for those with whom we minister models those qualities for them.

"**Take questions seriously.** Encourage questioning. Every question is an occasion for learning something new. If you do not have an answer, promise that you will make an effort to find one and then follow through.

"**Honor student's ideas.** Sometimes students have ideas that are different than our own. There is the possibility for God to work in our lives through the insights of our students. Discounting ideas can come across as discounting persons. Look upon every idea as a gift, and find a way to affirm the offering of that idea.

"**Encourage honest sharing.** Sometimes it is difficult for persons to share what they really think. Maybe they believe their perspective is not worthy of sharing with the group. Maybe they are offended by something someone else shared, but are not confident enough to address the issue. The unconditional love that God makes available to us through Jesus should allow all of us to respect the opinions of others, even if we do not agree. In this room are people from a number of different churches. We are able to be with one another because we have God's love in common. I doubt seriously that we would all agree on much else, but we can accept each other as children of God.

"**Use accessible language.** There are many ways we talk about God, the church, and each other. Remember that those who make up our classes come from a wide variety of backgrounds. Language that is understood and acceptable to some may offend or confuse others. Make sure you are clear and direct in what you say, translating church language into everyday terms that communicate with your audience.

Category: Class interaction
Take questions seriously
Honor students' ideas
Encourage honest sharing
Use accessible language

"The last category of caring is about caring for yourself and other teachers.

"**Take time to grow.** In our last session, we talked about the need to continue to grow as followers of Jesus. It is our growth, translated into our teaching situation, which communicates faith to those whom we teach. Worship, study, prayer, and service are all essential elements for us to grow in faith, and our growth is essential to the growth of our students. It is difficult for a student to surpass their teacher, so we must continue our faith journey if we want to help others along the way.

"**Support, encourage, and pray.** Pray for one another as teachers. Do you know the other teachers in your church? Do you meet together for training, support, and prayer? Maybe this is something you need to begin doing. It can be comforting to hear about the joy of another teacher when you are struggling. You may be able to provide new insight for a teacher about a particular person or topic. Together, you are stronger than you are as individuals. That strength can provide the foundation for a strong Sunday school throughout the lifespan of your congregation.

"**Take time off.** I need to heed this one myself! We need to allow time for rest and perspective, even if we love to teach. Give yourself a gift of time away from teaching to empower you for future teaching. God took time off when creation was completed. Jesus modeled times of Sabbath. We will certainly do well to follow their lead.

Category: Caring for yourself
Take time to grow
Support, encourage, and pray for other teachers
Take time off

"Tonight, I have done most of the talking," said Elizabeth. "I'd like to hear from you about what you are thinking in relation to the concept of teaching as a caring ministry."

"I think it's a great idea, but it seems like a lot more work. I'm just not sure I have any more time to put into what I do. Getting the lesson prepared and showing up on Sunday morning is about all I can handle right now." There were heads nodding agreement with this young mother's assessment.

Elizabeth was ready with her response. "Remember in the beginning of this session when I said caring is not just something we do, rather it becomes a part of who we are as a teacher? Here are a couple of ideas for you: Consider one or two of the ideas from this session that you think would make a difference in your class. Work on those. Soon you'll be doing them without even noticing. Then, add something else. Find some ways to involve others in expanding your caring ministry. Ask other class members to make follow-up calls. Each step along the way will make your class a more caring place. If you were here when we talked about using Appreciative Inquiry as a way of building on our strengths, you can see how that can be applied here. Start with what you already are doing and expand it."

"I have tried some of the ideas you've suggested, and the follow-up ideas have paid off big time. My attendance is much better when I call. I even call those who are there and let them know that I'm looking forward to seeing them on Sunday morning. It sure helps motivate my teens to get out of bed and get there!"

Another youth teacher offered her idea. "Most of my high school students have cell phones, and I have learned how to text up to ten of them at a time. It's a great way to use their technology to remind them that I care."

"We use e-mail to keep in touch in our adult class. It's become a reliable communication vehicle with many uses. I use it to check in, tell people about the lesson, and communicate a need or a joy. It's great!"

"Those are all great ideas, and we could go on all night, but I'm sure many of you need to get home and get some rest. Let's stand, make a circle around the room, and share concerns and joys." As the group did this, they didn't realize that this was Elizabeth's last effort to teach by modeling. When everyone had an opportunity to speak, she closed in a prayer that asked for God's attention and care upon each of these teachers and leaders who were responding to a call to provide caring ministry through the Sunday school.

After the closing "amen," she reminded them, "Next month will focus on a different model of Sunday morning educational ministry that is being used in one of our local congregations. I hope you'll be here."

10

Evaluate Needs

It seemed like a good time to get together. The workshops were going well, but the planning team wanted to be sure they continued to grow in the process. So they gathered again at Linda's church to discuss their accomplishments and make decisions about how to build on what had happened so far.

"I have to tell you I am seeing progress in my Sunday school because of the involvement of folks from my church in the workshops," volunteered Jim. "Attendance is up, and there just seems to be new life and excitement."

"We are using the Appreciative Inquiry process as we shape our Sunday school program," said Rachel. "We were already using it to identify strengths in starting our church, and it seem natural that we utilize the same process to build on those identified strengths, as we move to this new phase of our ministry."

Craig joined in. "We are also using Appreciative Inquiry. It has helped our Sunday school and church leaders see that we do have strengths. We are in the dreaming stage, just trying to figure out where God is calling is to go as we move forward. It's an exciting time at First Church."

"Teachers at my church have asked if we can form a Teacher's Class that meets an hour before Sunday school. They want to study together, touch base about family members in different classes, and have time to pray for one another and their classes." Elizabeth was beaming with pride. "The big news is that I am helping my new teaching partner find another partner, and I'm going to lead the Teacher's Class!"

"It sounds like we are accomplishing our goal of building on the strengths each church has in Sunday school to help all of our Sunday schools thrive. It's been especially good to see the number of people from our churches, as well as people from churches who haven't been a part of the planning for these workshops." Linda seemed to be emerging as the leader of the group. "Are we sure that the last two workshops are what we really need?"

Sue Munsey spoke up. "I'm excited about the intergenerational workshop that is scheduled next. I think many churches are so traditional that they struggle year after year trying to make age-level Sunday school work, when there are other ways to make something much more meaningful happen."

"I agree with you Sue," Linda said. "And I am looking forward to the last workshop that will give more options for how Sunday school can transition into the future in new forms. I just wonder if there is anything essential that we have left out? One area I've thought about is curriculum. Some of my leaders struggle with what I choose for them, but they really have no idea what they want or need."

Elizabeth added, "In the last workshop session, I heard several people mentioning that they thought they were going to get more help in the workshops on the actual teaching they do. A session on curriculum could sure address an important aspect of that."

"It sounds to me like we need to add another workshop," Craig commented. "Who would be able to provide the leadership for that session?"

"Well, I could check with our denominational bookstore about the curriculum specialist on their staff. He might be able to do it. Or, perhaps he could suggest someone else," said Linda.

"Sounds like a great idea to me, Linda, you being the professional and all." Jim affirmed.

"I don't know about that. I think everyone has done a professional job so far. I feel like I've learned a lot too," Linda responded. "So we will add one more workshop on the topic of curriculum. I'll let all of you know when I have secured a leader for the session. Jim, would you close this meeting with prayer for us?"

Jim Cantrell asked that everyone join him in prayer:

"Dear Lord, we are blessed by how you have used us so far in this adventure. It is exciting and we are thankful as we hear how the workshops have already started making differences in our own churches. May people come to know you, and live more fully in your saving grace, because of our Sunday school ministries. Lead us into the future, and allow the blessings to continue. We pray this seeking the guidance of the Great Teacher, your son, Jesus. Amen."

With Jim's prayer as their benediction, the group members went their own ways.

Thoughts Along the Path

Take a few moments to reflect on what you have read in *Sacred Challenge* so far.

Have you tried any of the ideas you have read about?

Is there one concept or new idea that stands out for you or your Sunday school situation?

How have you been reminded of God working through your Sunday school?

What other topic would you want to see included?

11

Generations

Sue Munsey came prepared, knowing that her topic tonight would be a challenge to communicate. She had been one of the advocates for trying something different in her church, and without a defined process like Appreciative Inquiry, navigating the passage from traditional age-level Sunday school to something new had been difficult. It was always important to remember that the years leading up to the change had also held significant challenge.

Her church of seventy members struggled with their Sunday school. Every year, finding teachers required greater effort. Everyone in the small church felt they had already served their time, and thought it was someone else's turn. Those who finally did step forward did so out of a sense of duty, and saw teaching as one more thing to survive during their hectic weeks. Once the teachers were finally in place, it was difficult to keep them. The junior and senior high class would have four teens on a good Sunday, but more often had one or two, with some weeks being totally absent of students. There was little motivation for teachers to do significant preparation, and on Sundays when there were no students were present, they complained about why a class was even offered. The children's class was not much better attended, and adults didn't come to Sunday school because the pastor led it. They were going to hear him or her in worship just after Sunday school. The end result was a Sunday school program with about twenty-five people on a good Sunday, and around fifteen on a regular basis. Tonight, Sue would share about the journey into intergenerational Sunday school.

When people had arrived and were settling into their chairs, Sue began. "Welcome to our fifth workshop. Tonight, I want to share a quote that I've heard referred to as 'the seven last words of the church.' Then I'm going to suggest a new way of thinking about Sunday school that will blow that phrase apart! The quote I'm referring to goes like this: 'We've never done it that way before.'" Laughter erupted from the crowd. Sue continued, "It's easy for us to laugh now, but when something threatens what we see as important and essential, we might find ourselves saying that very phrase,' or something similar.

"How many of you are in churches where traditional, age-level Sunday school classes are offered?" Everyone except people from Sue's church and St. Andrews (Linda's church) raised their hands. "I thought so. How many of you who raised your hands are ready to completely scrap what you are doing and move on to something totally different for Sunday school?" Three hands were raised. Sue expected this response and was ready with her own.

"Tonight, we are going to explore a whole new way of doing Sunday school. While it may seem radical—it certainly was for us when our church went to this approach several years back—it may be better than struggling with your current way of doing Sunday school just because it is the way you always did Sunday school. The other option may be to disband the Sunday school altogether. I know some churches are considering this as a possibility.

"My church decided to try the radical approach of intergenerational Sunday school because the old way was no longer working, and we didn't want to lose Sunday school altogether. I am sure you are already asking yourself or a neighbor, 'What does she mean by intergenerational Sunday school?' That is a great question, and together we will try to answer it by the end of this session.

"If you look around you will see that we have an even greater diversity of ages here tonight than we have had at our previous workshops. I have asked some members of my church to join us and talk about who they are from an age standpoint. To do this, we have used something called 'generational theory.' We've always known that each generation had uniqueness, but in 1991 Neil Howe and William Strauss published a book called *Generations: The History of America's Future 1584-2069* (San Francisco: Harper). In this groundbreaking book, Howe and Strauss combined social anthropology and political history to identify recurring patterns in generations throughout the history of America. I have asked five people to speak to you briefly about who they are, and tell you a little about their generation. Jennifer will be our first speaker."

"Hi. As Sue mentioned, I am Jennifer. I am one of the oldest members of our church, and I am a member of the G.I. Generation. Most of us were born during World War I, survived the Depression, World War II, and several other wars and conflicts. People from my generation typically want everyone to be involved and agree—think about how that works in your church—and we want people to have meaningful faith experiences in structured settings. We G.I. generation folks believe in doing your duty, and so I was one of the people who taught Sunday school year after year because nobody else would. I'm involved in our intergenerational Sunday school, and though it gets a little rowdy sometimes, I really enjoy it."

"My name is Jeff. I am a part of the Silent Generation. My generation believes in working hard and doing your duty. Most of the mainline denominations came about because of my generation's work to provide stability for the church and future members. We get the most out of faith when we are doing something. Most of that doing relates to our desire for a strong structure for the future.

We're not so crazy about change, and when this intergenerational idea came around, I have to tell you I didn't like it at first. Fortunately, Sue and others have let me work with structuring the new Sunday school at our church, and I have really liked my part in making something new work."

"I am Sandy, and I am a Boomer! We're the most studied group of people on the planet. It seems like everyone in the world has wanted to find out what makes us tick, and specifically how we spend our money. I do have to say that my G.I. generation parents are aghast at how much we spent on our house and how many credit cards we have. There weren't very many Boomers at our church when we made the change to Intergeneration Sunday school, but I was ready for a change and led the initial planning group for the new program. The change has been nothing but positive, and a number of our friends have recognized the visionary leadership it took to make this transition. Some have joined us on this new journey."

"My name is Blake, I am one of the dreaded Gen Xers! My generation has had a difficult time with anything institutional, and we have spent most of our adult life trying to find unconventional ways to relate to God. I would have never gone to our church before the change, and sometimes I wish we could just be a little looser in how we do things. The reality is I've learned a lot from people of different ages in our intergenerational Sunday school, and I think I have even had some influence on its direction. The best part of this experiment has been establishing some really cool relationships with people older and younger than me. If we could just get a little more of this experiential stuff into our worship, I would really like it."

"Hello, I'm Hillary and I'm in ninth grade. You'll also be glad to know that I am the last speaker! I am part of the Generation Y, or Millennial Generation, or the Bridger Generation. They have lots of names for us, and we are probably studied even more than my parents' Boomer generation. According to the marketing world, we have spending power greater than any other generation because we tell our parents how to spend their money! I'm not so sure mine always listen, but I keep telling them anyway. We Gen Ys want to

make the world a better place, so I get to help with the mission out-
reach programs that are a part of our intergenerational Sunday
school. That's the most exciting part for me. I learn about Jesus'
example and know that he lives through my life so I can make this
a better world."

Generations
G.I 1900 – 1925
Silents 1925 – 1942
Boomers 1943 – 1962
Gen X 1962 – 1982
Gen Y 1982 – 2005
*Time periods are approximate and are not agreed upon
by all generational experts.

Sue came back to the front to address the participants. "You
have now heard from the five generations that populate the church
and our world today. You heard a few characteristics and gained a
little insight into our intergenerational Sunday school, expressed
from each generational viewpoint. I want to allow you a few minutes, in twos or threes, to discuss what you know about people in
each age group. Do you think the descriptions you heard here
tonight ring true? Take about ten minutes, and then we'll come
back together as one group to continue."

At the end of the allotted time, Sue called the group back
together. "Let's hear from your conversations. What do you think
about 'generational theory?'"

"You know, young lady, I think this is a bunch of hooey. Why,
I could find somebody with all of them same things to say in any
age group." Having had his say, the older gentleman leaned back in
his chair, crossed his arms over his large barrel chest, and looked
like he was daring anyone to say differently.

Sue was ready. "You are exactly right. It is important, any time
we talk in general about a group of people, to recognize that there
are exceptions. What has been helpful about the generational theory
for us is that there are some general trends that can provide a path

of understanding for the majority of people in an age group. The planning group for our new Sunday school used this information to help blaze our new path. While the information isn't totally conclusive, it is informative."

"I was struck by how there seems to be similarities between some of the older generations and younger generations. It seems like the G.I.s have some common ground with the Gen Y folks."

"This is true. There is a cyclical nature to generational theory, so we should expect the same kind of relationship between the Silents and the generation that follows Generation Y. This does pave the way for some great relationships between generations."

"These theories sound great, but how in the world are you able to do something worthwhile in an educational setting with that much diversity of age?" At last a Silent Generation member voiced the concerns that must have been shared by all of the Silents who were present.

"I am so glad you asked that question. It will provide a transition to the next part of our session tonight. Let's take a short break, and then we'll move on to learning more about intergenerational learning."

As Sue called the group back together after the break, she asked participants to get into five groups. Each group had one of the representatives from her church present. Sue also encouraged the groups to divide into mixed age groups as much as possible. Since there were about fifty people present, the groups had about ten people in each.

Sue asked that each group choose a leader by determining who had a birthday closest to the present. There was a great deal of lively chatter as each group tried to do the math needed to figure out who would be their leader. Next, Sue instructed the groups to take a few minutes to share at least one thing they had learned since they arrived tonight. She listened and discovered that most people had no idea that there was something called generational theory. Having the members of her congregation share with them was enlightening to most attendees.

The groups were becoming more comfortable with each other, so Sue moved on to the next step in her process. "I would like you to go around your group one more time and allow each person to share the place they feel closest to God." Silence fell on the group for a full minute, and then one by one, group leaders started to share.

"In my back yard." "At the sea shore. "When I'm alone in the sanctuary at my church." "Standing by my baby's crib when she is sleeping." The sharing went on and provided a kaleidoscope of ways that people, in the room of all ages, experienced God.

As the sharing faded, signaling that each group had completed its task, Sue gave more instructions. "I would like to have the leader ask for a volunteer to pray for the members of each group. Include in your prayer thanksgiving for the ability to learn something new, and for places where we can feel God's presence in a special way." Most groups joined hands as they bowed in prayer. Before long, groups were beginning to chat again as they completed their prayers.

"Now, if I can have your attention back up front," Sue requested. "How did you feel about what you just experienced?"

"It was great, I learned more about the people I have been seeing at these workshops."

"I felt privileged to be involved in my group. It was really a holy time for me."

"Having different ages present allowed us to hear perspectives we might not get otherwise."

"I think you are beginning to see the possibilities. What you just experienced was a miniature intergenerational event. Granted, things are a little noisier at our place with children of different ages present. We do more with a theme or lesson when we have an hour rather than a few minutes. I just wanted you to see that it is possible to have meaningful time learning together in a setting that crosses age boundaries.

"In most of our churches, as soon as we enter the door, families go their separate ways. This is because the way we currently do Sunday school in most churches harkens back to age-level classifications in school systems. Prior to that time, both in public and

Sunday school, groupings were more inclusive of different ages. At our church, we have reversed that trend.

"We struggled with low numbers and had difficulty finding teachers. We finally decided we had to do something. It's hard to maintain anything meaningful without consistency on the part of students and teachers. That's when we formed the group that you heard Sandy speak about earlier. Since we didn't have anyone with training at our church, we asked Linda French to work with us on a new plan. Her help was invaluable. She guided us to the realization that, as a small church, the greatest strength we possessed was our sense of family. We began to discuss how we could turn that strength into a new form of Sunday school. The intergenerational approach was perfect. We were actually doing something very similar to the Appreciative Inquiry process without knowing it.

"At first, there were challenges related to finding curriculum that worked for us. It was also hard to figure out a leadership process that allowed everyone to be participants as well as leaders. Our morning schedule changed due to our minister's responsibility at another church. Linda helped us find curriculum, we worked out a rotation for leadership, and the schedule actually became a gift in disguise! The church has been doing this style of Sunday school for two years now, and we have no regrets.

"Oh, I also wanted to tell you that instead of averaging fifteen people in Sunday school each week, we now average forty! Sunday morning Christian education has become a life-long journey at our church—one that happens every Sunday."

One person, who raised his hand earlier when Sue asked if they would be willing to try something different for Sunday school, raised his hand again.

"Yes?" Sue asked.

"Can you give us an idea of what happens in one of your sessions?"

"Sure, but remember this is like a snapshot. On a different Sunday morning with a different leader, what happens could be entirely unique. That's part of what makes this fun. Anyway, here's an example of a session:

"Most of us come to Sunday school from our worship service, so coffee, juice, and a snack is available. This gives everyone time to check in with each other and get a little something to keep them going. About ten minutes into the hour, some music begins. Sometimes the music is guitar, sometimes piano, sometimes it is recorded. That is the signal for everyone to find a seat. There is a welcome, we sing a couple of songs, and celebrate any special events like birthdays or anniversaries. Then we have a prayer time. Sometimes the leader prays, and sometimes there is a prayer posted on the wall for everyone to read together. My favorite is when one of the children or a family prays for us. At this point, there is a special activity for everyone. We may hear a story, watch a video clip, or someone may act out a passage of scripture. Whatever it is, the activity is a focus for the rest of the session. Following this, there are learning activities. The group may break up into smaller units and visit different stations in the room. They may all be doing the same learning activity in different parts of the room. This has been one of the things we've had to learn. We thought that adults would be bored with some of the art or craft activities. Instead, they love it! There aren't many places where adults are allowed to get their fingers into paint, or do sculpture with modeling clay. We are finding this a favorite part of the program for adults. They also have been surprised by the insights children in the group have shared through these activities. We really can learn from children if we are open to that possibility. In the end, we come back together as a total group to share joys and concerns, and then pray together. Remember that this may be a general pattern, but there are many variations on the pattern. It's part of what makes this style interesting. Any questions?"

"How much did it cost you to make the change?" asked an older gentleman.

"Actually, we are paying less for curriculum and using a few more materials, so that is about the same. The addition of snacks is really the only new cost, and we put out a basket to recoup those costs. So far it seems to work."

"How do you coordinate the leadership?"

"The planning team meets once a quarter. We look at curriculum, choose topics, and assign responsibilities. Assignments seem to happen naturally because of gifts or interest. We know we can call on other members of the team if we need help. The leadership really happens by family instead of individual. That is another plus for this style of Sunday school: It involves everyone."

"Do you think this is just a fad, and you'll go back to normal Sunday school in the future?"

"This has become normal Sunday school for us. We made this change because what had been 'normal' was no longer working for our congregation. There could be a time in the future when this needs to change also. I hope we never get so locked into one style that we let Sunday school die instead of modifying what we do and how we do it."

Are you willing to make a change rather than letting your Sunday school die for lack of faith that God can work through a new style of ministry?

Linda said, "I want to thank you and the members of your congregation who have shared with us tonight. I feel more open to trying something new than I ever have in the past. I think if your congregation can make this shift, mine can too. I for one think it's high time we look at doing just that. You've mentioned the Appreciative Inquiry process several times. Until now, I didn't see how it could be useful in our situation. Now I can see how a church can discover its strength, dream up something new, and then make it happen. Thanks for being such a powerful example."

"Well thank you for that statement," said Sue. "Passing on what we've learned is one more way we can thank God for the changes this has brought about in our church. Please give me a call if you have any further questions concerning anything we've discussed tonight.

"Before we close, I also want to remind you that next month, Linda will be leading us in a workshop designed to help us understand how we grow and learn. That session will offer additional alternative styles of Sunday morning Christian education. I also want to announce that we have decided to add one more workshop to this series. Our last workshop will be in two months, and will be everything you always wanted to know about choosing and using curriculum. We have secured the leadership of a denominational curriculum specialist for that session.

"Let's join in a closing prayer circle." As the participants circled the room, they shared joys and challenges that faced them and those they loved. Jennifer, from Sue's church, closed with a beautiful prayer:

"Oh God of love, we are thankful to be gathered together to learn more about being in ministry to all of your children, wherever they are in life. May we drop our preconceived ideas about the young, the old, and all those in between, so that together we can discover your call on our lives. In discovering that call, give us the strength to respond. You know our joys, and you know our needs. Be present in our lives and those lives we lift to you, working your miracle of love in each heart.

"We love you, God. We need you, and we seek to serve you. Go with us, allowing us to live out our destiny as your people. In the name of Jesus, we pray, amen."

12

The Ways We Learn

This month's workshop would be a challenge, Linda realized. Most of the people who had attended the last session on intergenerational Sunday school were involved in churches where traditional Sunday school was the norm. Even by the end of Sue's presentation, there seemed to be few who were interested in trying something different.

The lack of willingness to move out of a traditional structure for Sunday school, when most of the churches present were experiencing less and less participation, surprised Linda. St. Andrews had been in that mode when she arrived. Sunday school attendance had leveled off several years earlier and was beginning to shrink. The church had recognized the importance of this ministry, and had asked pointed questions during her interview about how Linda would revive involvement. Her answer had been to share what she knew about how people process information. She shared why traditional Sunday school methods left room for growth to enable children, youth, and adults greater involvement in their learning experiences.

The church accepted Linda's premise, and the Sunday school at St. Andrews now looked remarkably different than it had when she arrived. Involvement levels continued to rise, and effective, meaningful, enjoyable Sunday school had become a major reason that younger families were being attracted to her church. Linda's challenge tonight would be to convince people attending this session that they too could lead a transformation in the way learning takes place in their setting.

As people arrived they were given a catalog from Linda's church, describing all of the offerings for adults. These included traditional classes on Sunday morning, short-term topical studies, long-term Bible studies offered on Sunday mornings, as well as other times during the week. A brochure describing children's Sunday school, and a fact sheet about youth Sunday school, were also in the information each participant received. As in the past, members of the planning team greeted each person as they arrived and invited them to find a seat.

"Tonight's session will focus on alternative possibilities for Sunday school. As you heard at our last workshop, the current structure of most Sunday schools is derived from a public school model that places people in groups based on ages. There are different ways of understanding how we grow mentally, socially, and spiritually that should cause us to consider new frames of reference for how people are grouped for ministry. We will be looking at information related to the development of our brains tonight, and that information, which is more recent than the Sunday school structure used in most of our churches, has the possibility of pointing us in some new directions.

"I am excited that there are so many of you here tonight. I look forward to sharing some insights that have guided St. Andrews to new places in our Sunday morning educational ministry.

"On the screen, you will see some information related to how our brains develop.

Brain Development
> At Birth—25% of adult size
> First 48 months critical in brain development
> Visual and tactile stimulation is vital in the first year
> Brain is 85-90% of adult size by age 5
> Reading and writing is important to development at this age
> Continued visual, auditory, and tactile stimulation helps the brain develop
> Brain "connectors" expand in the right brain first (4-7yrs.)
> Brain "connectors" expand in the left side next (9-12yrs.)
> Brain is ready for abstract thinking about 13 years of age
> "Pruning" (refining) of connections continues through adulthood

(*Teaching With The Brain In Mind*, Eric Jensen, Association for Supervision and curriculum Development, Alexandria, VA 1998.)

"Looking at the information on the screen, we can see that there is a lot going on during childhood and adolescence in relation to brain development. You might be asking, 'Why do I need to know all of this? I'm just a Sunday school teacher, not a brain expert!' The reality is we can learn a great deal about how to effectively share the stories of our faith—even the very essence of our faith—by understanding how our brains work. We can also help children become the people God created them to be by providing the right learning environments and teaching activities.

"I've asked a friend to read a passage of scripture that reminds us that our creation is not just a biological process. God is intimately involved in every aspect of development."

Jerry Hall from St. Andrews walked to the front of the room and began to read:

> I praise you, for I am fearfully and wonderfully made.
>   Wonderful are your works;
> that I know very well.
>   My frame was not hidden from you,
> when I was being made in secret,
>   intricately woven in the depths of the earth.
> Your eyes beheld my unformed substance.
> In your book were written
>   all the days that were formed for me,
>   when none of them as yet existed.
> How weighty to me are your thoughts, O God!
>   How vast is the sum of them!   (Psalms 139:14-17)

"Thanks, Jerry. I think this passage tells us that even during week three of our embryonic development, when our brain was just becoming a distinguishable part of our physical make-up, God was involved. It is a precious trust that God has afforded us, to help in the development of this splendid gift.

"As you can see from our chart on the screen, there are many ways we can enhance God's creation as it is found in the children we work with in Sunday school. Children need to be exposed to a variety of differing stimuli. Hugs, stories, drama, crafts, art, and music all have a place in the enrichment of this amazing gift from God. Brain researchers tell us that we can actually influence how a brain develops, depending on how we enable it to interact with others and with the world. We'll look at some specific ways to do this through new forms of Sunday school shortly.

"Before we do that, I want to show you a ten minute video clip about teenage brain development.

"The Teen Brain"
(http://www.pbs.org/newshour/bb
/science/july-dec04/brain_10-13.html)

Key Points

Teen brains are different than adult brains.

The prefrontal cortex, which controls impulse behaviors and decision-making, is not developed fully until about twenty-five.

Brain connections "thin out" during adolescence determining thinking patterns for the rest of our lives.

Adults and teens use different parts of their brains for making decisions. Adults use visuals, teens use cognitive.

"Any ideas about the implications for what we can do in Sunday school with teens, given what we just watched?"

"It just confirms what I've always thought. When you ask a teen 'what were you thinking,' the answer is that they weren't! Now I know that they can't!"

"I think it does mean that we need to be more patient with them and remember to accept them where they are."

"It sounds like we can help them develop their brains by challenging them to think."

"We should give them more time to respond. It's easy to just fill in the silence with our own voice when they don't answer immediately. It sounds like it takes them longer to process information, so we should give them more time."

"From the information you shared with us earlier, it sounds like we can explore more conceptual ideas with teens in the classroom."

"You have come up with some great ideas for teaching youth, given their brain development," Linda commented. "As one of you said, this research just confirms some things those of us who have raised teens already knew. Their ability to think about the consequence of their actions just isn't there yet. That has some implications for how we do Sunday school. There also are some clues for us in relation to how we do adult Sunday school. Check out this next slide.

Our brains are fully developed by about age twenty-five.

Adults process information related to visual imagery.

Researchers tell us that the "pruning" process continues throughout our lifetime.

While our brain begins to lose cells every day after we reach twenty years old, it still generates new materials after sixty to compensate for some that is lost. Our ability does slow down as we become older.
(http://www.pfizer.com/brain/etour3.htm)

The pruning process referred to here is the process of how the neurons in our brain are connected. As these are refined, we are able to more easily think about an issue or topic in a predetermined way. This speeds our response time, but may limit our ability to think "outside the box."

"We can see that there are a number of implications for how we do teaching and learning with adults in different stages of life. One implication is that the most standard form of adult education—lecture—may not be the most effective. For example, if you are trying to help adults understand a new concept, and you know that adults process information by relating information received to stored images, you also need to know that they will require a new image. Otherwise, they will translate the new information into established images. We'll look together soon at how that might be done.

"I want to share one more bit of brain information with you before we get to the practical part of tonight's session. Harvard professor Howard Gardner developed this information. If you look on the screen, you will see descriptions of what he calls 'multiple intelligences.'

"I would like to ask you to take a few minutes with someone sitting next to you to discuss which of these resonates with how you experience the world and process information. You may find that you relate to more than one."

People jumped into the conversation, anxious to discuss what they saw as their way of relating to information and their world.

Howard Gardner initially formulated a list of eight intelligences. His listing was provisional. The first two are ones that have been typically valued in schools; the next three are usually associated with the arts; and the final two are what Howard Gardner called personal intelligences Gardner, Howard (1999) *Intelligence Reframed. Multiple intelligences for the 21st century*, New York: Basic Books, pp 41-43.

Linguistic intelligence involves sensitivity to spoken and written language, the ability to learn languages, and the capacity to use language to accomplish certain goals. This intelligence includes the ability to effectively use language to express oneself rhetorically or poetically; and language as a means to remember information. Writers, poets, lawyers and speakers are among those who Howard Gardner sees as having high linguistic intelligence.

Logical-mathematical intelligence consists of the capacity to analyze problems logically, carry out mathematical operations, and investigate issues scientifically. In Howard Gardner's words, it entails the ability to detect patterns, reason deductively, and think logically. This intelligence is most often associated with scientific and mathematical thinking.

Musical intelligence involves skill in the performance, composition, and appreciation of musical patterns. It encompasses the capacity to recognize and compose musical pitches, tones, and rhythms. According to Howard Gardner musical intelligence runs in an almost structural parallel to linguistic intelligence.

Bodily-kinesthetic intelligence entails the potential of using one's whole body or parts of the body to solve problems. It is the ability to use mental abilities to coordinate bodily movements. Howard Gardner sees mental and physical activity as related.

Spatial intelligence involves the potential to recognize and use the patterns of wide space and more confined areas.

Interpersonal intelligence is concerned with the capacity to understand the intentions, motivations and desires of other people. It allows people to work effectively with others. Educators, salespeople, religious and political leaders, and counselors all need a well-developed interpersonal intelligence.

Intrapersonal intelligence entails the capacity to understand oneself, to appreciate one's feelings, fears, and motivations. In Howard Gardner's view, it involves having an effective working model of ourselves, and to be able to use such information to regulate our lives.

What "intelligence" best describes how you relate to your world?

Which "intelligence" best relates to the way you teach Sunday school?

"All right," Linda said. "Let's take an inventory. I would like to ask you to raise your hand when I call out the intelligence that you feel most closely reflects your personal way of interacting with your world."

Linda went through the list. By the end of the exercise, everyone had found himself or herself described by one of Gardner's intelligences. Every category had at least several people represented in the group.

"As you have seen, every category of intelligence is represented in this group. Multiply that by the number of Sunday school students in all of our churches. What does this mean for us as we plan for Sunday school sessions?" Linda asked.

"I think it means that whatever we do, we're leaving someone out," was the first response.

"It reminds me of our last workshop, when we experienced a number of different ways to encounter God and each other."

"I need to completely rethink how I engage adults in my class. I thought all I needed to do was get them thinking. Now I realize that getting them thinking has a lot more possibilities than throwing out some good questions about a passage of scripture."

"I knew that seeing this information would break open your thinking about how we teach," said Linda. "I want to spend the rest of our time together looking at some possibilities for structuring Sunday school to allow a broader spectrum of growth for the people God has blessed us with as students. First, let's look at children's ministry.

"We know that we can influence the development of our children's brains by providing them with a variety of experiences. Our church has found that both stimulation of thought and retention of information can be better accomplished through an alternative to traditional Sunday school. When I came to St. Andrews, Sunday school attendance was going down in every age group. Children's classrooms were boring, and I was hearing from parents that their children felt bored as well. Teachers felt overwhelmed by the curriculum and reverted to what they had done before because it was easier.

"In our research, we discovered the workshop rotation model. It was started in a church in the Chicago area that dealt with the same issues we were. It seemed like a great option for us. Check out the screen for a description of the model.

> Here's the workshop rotation model in a nutshell: Teach major Bible stories and concepts through kid-friendly multimedia workshops: an art workshop, drama, music, games, audio-visuals, puppets, storytelling, computers, and any other educational media you can get your hands on. Teach the same Bible story in all of the workshops for four or five weeks, rotating the kids to a different workshop each week. And here comes the extremely teacher friendly part: Keep the same teacher in each workshop for all five weeks, teaching the same lesson week after week (with some age appropriate adjustments) to each new class coming in. (http://www.rotation.org/outlook.htm)

"The result was that everyone loved it. We made modifications that worked for us. We only offer four options most of the time and group children accordingly. We have guides who are with the children every week to promote continuity. We choose the Bible stories that reflect themes our pastor is using for sermons during the same time period.

"Attendance has gone up. Leaders are more willing to teach for four weeks at a time because they only prepare once. Guides love getting to know their group without having to also prepare a lesson. We think we are doing a better job of connecting children with their faith, each other, and caring adults. We believe that we are also stimulating new ways for them to use their brains to develop spiritually.

"What questions do you have about this concept?"

"How could we use this in a church with only ten children? I love it, but it looks like something that works for a large church and isn't realistic for many of us."

"I can understand how it would look difficult to do with a smaller church. Maybe you only have one class, but work toward utilizing a different method to teach the same Bible story over the period of a month. Perhaps you have four teachers who teach only once each month. The intergenerational model may work better in your congregation.

"What I really want to do is start a thinking process that allows you to consider reshaping what you are currently doing. The traditional Sunday school class needs to give way to new possibilities for the future. I believe that if you make changes that incorporate more of what we know about how God created us to think and respond, you will also grow your Sunday school. I want to remind you of the Appreciative Inquiry process as a resource for building on the strengths that already exist in your particular congregation."

"Where do you get curriculum to use in the rotation model?"

"That was difficult at first, but most denominational publishers now have curriculum available. Just remember: Any curriculum needs some adaptation to a local congregation's needs. You can discover more about how to do that in the final workshop next month."

"This sounds really exciting. How do I get started?"

"Begin by talking to others at your church. You might want to visit a church that is using this model. There are churches in almost every area of the country doing the workshop rotation model. We would be honored to have you visit us one Sunday morning. The transition is a challenge, and you may need to begin to use the concept in your current structure. Another option is to completely shut down what you are doing long enough to make the change. This can actually build excitement for the 'new' Sunday school.

"If there are no further questions, I'd like to spend a few minutes talking about youth Sunday school. This is probably one of the biggest challenges we face. Just as youth are becoming able better to grasp the conceptual nature of faith, they are also being given more freedom to decide where and how they will be involved in the church. Unfortunately, many of our youth and youth families see confirmation as a graduation from the church, rather than a deeper commitment to the church. Our youth Sunday school attendance was abysmal. The classes were boring. Teachers either took sharing the concepts of the faith as permission to lecture, allowing youth no opportunity to utilize their developing brainpower, or they didn't believe that the youth would respond to faith issues. Often, they ended up talking about Friday night's football game. Our youth were happy with neither. They said they wanted to understand more about the Bible, the church, and how to be a follower of Jesus, but they wanted it to relate to real life. Oh, and they also wanted it to be fun.

"After a number of interviews with youth and parents, we started looking around. What we found were youth Sunday schools that were traditional, where the youth arrived and sat in chairs, while someone 'taught' them from the front of the room. We found a variation on the theme, where teachers were good at engaging youth in conversation, but still used the concept of having information that they needed to share with the youth. We found big groups who had music and prayer and almost a mini-sermon as the teaching for the morning. It was almost like a separate youth worship service.

"It was decided that we needed to create a whole new way of doing youth Sunday school. We found leaders who wanted to teach, but weren't great at relating to youth. We found leaders who had a gift for relating to youth, but didn't have time to prepare a lesson every week. We had a young adult who loved anything to do with media, but wasn't old enough to be a youth leader. We put those people together, and this is what we created.

"As youth arrive, there is music playing that provides a backdrop for the theme of the morning. Sometimes, there may even be a video, depending on the topic. All youth gather in one room for about ten minutes of direct teaching. Our media guy and the teacher coordinate to present the topic in a creative way. This means that there might be a song, video clip, or short drama to illustrate the key concept of the morning. After this presentation, youth divide into small groups led by relational leaders. The main teacher provides an outline that is process driven for groups to use in their time together. The small group leader is responsible for working through the outline and getting to know youth on a personal level. This allows what the group is talking about to become more applicable to the lives of the individuals in that particular group. At the end of the hour, all of the groups meet back together to share what they have learned in a creative way. This is the favorite time for many of our youth, and some of the role-plays, television commercials, songs, drawings, and sculptures relate the topic of the day to the lives of our youth in hilariously innovative ways. They end up learning more from each other than from the teacher. The group ends in a prayer circle, sharing concerns and joys.

"Small group leaders make contact with members of their group who were absent. The new format, along with our emphasis on caring, has quadrupled the number of youth in Sunday school! We believe this format, just as in children's Sunday school, utilizes the God-given gifts of our leaders and students, allowing them to discover new relationships with God and others.

"I know many of you are thinking, 'How can we do that with three, five, or ten youth?' The answer may be that this is not the answer for you. Or maybe you start with one small group and apply the principles of building relationships and involving youth in their own learning differently in your setting. The key is not whether you do youth Sunday school like St. Andrews, but that you respond to where youth are in life. Do what you can to include them in the discovery of their place among the people of God.

"We do have youth who have chosen a different way of growing through Sunday school. They are guides for our children's ministry. I hear from them that they learn as much as the children during their journeys through our rotation model. I have heard of other churches where youth help teach children's classes in other ways. And, don't forget the intergenerational Sunday school model. It may work better than an age-level model in your church.

"I hope this gives you some ideas for a new path for youth Sunday school in your setting.

"I want to quickly move to adult Sunday school. What models do you use in your church presently?"

"They sit. I talk," said one of the teachers from a small church nearby.

"Mine isn't much different. We have a fellowship time, and then we get down to the lesson. The teacher makes a presentation and people respond. We do have some lively discussion."

"Remember the variety of intelligences we saw represented in the room earlier? If we take seriously the information that adults relate to their world and information in a wide variety of ways, we need to provide a wide variety of structures and settings for that learning to take place.

"Lecturing may be a great way to communicate some information to some of your class members, but what about that freedom Sue told us about when adults get to finger paint? How do we structure our Sunday school for adults, as well as children and youth, so everyone can find new meaning in the Good News? I think you will find that some of the teachers who volunteer with children and youth, some of you in this room, have chosen to do so because the way learning happens in those settings more closely relates to how you process information. This is not a matter of intelligence, but a matter of learning style. It's a matter of how God wired your brain in the creation process.

"We are experimenting with a comprehensive approach to adult education that involves a variety of topics and styles. If you look at the catalog you received tonight, you can see some of the offerings. This catalog includes Sunday morning classes, as well as other learning activities and groups. We do have traditional adult classes on Sunday morning. We also offer short-term topical studies, and long-term Bible studies. We are trying to vary our approach by seeking input from a variety of adults in the congregation.

"One of our Bible studies is video based and class members share leadership. One short-term class is an art class, which seeks to celebrate the holy as we discover it in God's creation. The idea is to respond to the ways our particular adults can discover and relate to God. This approach seems to span the age spectrum, from young adults to older adults. When we join this with our children and youth offerings, we have truly created a life-long learning environment.

"This is a different way of accomplishing the same thing Sue's church has done through their intergenerational class. Once more, I am not suggesting that your Sunday school should look like ours. What I am suggesting is that your Sunday school should reflect the people God has gathered together in your church. Any comments?"

"I am tremendously impressed by what you have accomplished at your church. To be honest, I am a little overwhelmed. Where I see hope for my small congregation, is in using a process like Appreciative Inquiry, taking the generational information from the last workshop, the brain development information from this one, and discovering some new ways to connect people of all ages with the faith. Thanks for your help tonight."

"I would echo what we just heard, and add that I didn't think my church could really do anything except what we have always done in Sunday school and hope for the best. What I am beginning to believe is that we can't be satisfied with being comfortable. I think God really is calling us to be on the cutting edge."

"Your affirmations confirm that those of us who got together eight months ago were responding to a call from God and our churches. As we continue to learn and grow together, God will surely bless what we strive to accomplish for the faith. I want to thank all of you for coming tonight, and ask that we take a few minutes in silence to consider where we are being called from here."

After a short period of silence, Linda closed the evening with an appropriate prayer. As people were starting toward the door, she reminded them about the final workshop to be held on the first Tuesday of next month.

Thoughts Along the Path

What reactions do you have to the presentation Linda made about their alternative styles of Sunday school?

How do you see the brain research and multiple intelligence information helping you determine how Sunday school could be more effective in your setting?

What new ideas do you have for your Sunday school ministry?

13

Teaching People

Tom Blakley had worked with his publishing company for a number of years. Originally, he was a young seminarian whose professor submitted some of his work to an editor friend for feedback. The editor liked Tom's work, and an ongoing relationship was established for the first ten years of Tom's local church ministry. By day, Tom provided church leadership as a local pastor. Nights and weekends were spent sporadically writing curriculum resources for his denomination.

As time went on, Tom was approached about becoming a field editor. He edited material from home, and worked with young curriculum resource writers as they developed an understanding of how the materials moved from a concept to a published reality. He found that he was always willing to subjugate parish responsibilities to writing, editing, and working with other writers. He decided that God was moving him in this direction for full-time ministry. About the same time, the publishing arm of his denomination saw the need for curriculum specialists to serve the church throughout the country. A lack of understanding about how to select and use resources was leading to criticism of those resources. The recommendation was to establish people like Tom Blakley in areas of the country where they already lived to serve as resources to both denominational bookstores and to the church in their particular areas.

Because of his path into this job, Tom was a perfect candidate for the last workshop of this series. When Linda contacted him, Tom was somewhat surprised by the nature of the workshops. He often provided leadership for local churches and groups of churches from his denomination, but he rarely had been invited to the type of cross-denominational setting Linda told him about. It was an unusual phenomena, and he was anxious to see what was happening in these gatherings. Tom quickly agreed and the time was now here for his workshop, the final of the series.

The topic must have been one that people wanted, because the room was packed. Tom was amazed. According to Linda French, there were almost one hundred people present, and over twenty churches represented.

Linda opened the session. "I want to welcome each of you to our final session tonight. This is by far the largest turnout to date, and I'm curious. I would like to hear why you chose to be a part of this particular workshop."

A hand shot up in the middle of the group, "I have been here for the last four of the workshops, and have been really impressed with what I've been able to learn. I just didn't want to miss the last one."

"This is my first time to attend, but I've been hearing from friends in other churches about the great stuff that has been going on. I wanted to get in on at least one."

"Well," it was the older, barrel-chested man from an earlier session. "I've been to almost all of the workshops. They were interesting, but it sounded like this one on curriculum was one that would give me some practical help. That's why I'm here tonight."

"On behalf of the planning committee, I want to thank and welcome each of you. We have a special treat tonight. Our leader is a man far more experienced with our topic of curriculum than any of us. Tom Blakley has been a local church pastor, curriculum resource writer, and an editor. Now he specializes in helping local churches and groups like ours understand more about curriculum, how it is developed, and how we can use it most effectively. Tom, we welcome you."

"Thanks, Linda," Tom began. "I think this is one of the largest groups I've worked with. I guess you know that the ecumenical nature of this group harkens back to the early days before the beginning of the 1900s, when the Sunday school was an organization beyond local churches. All that to say, I'm impressed with what you are doing here, and hope my presence can further your goal of making your Sunday schools more effective places to connect participants with our Christian faith.

"When I first started writing curriculum resources, I had a meeting with my editor. He asked me about flexibility in the materials I had written. I told him that if teachers left anything out, or used it differently than it was intended, there would be serious consequences. He looked at me strangely and asked if I was planning to have spies in each church that used my curriculum. At first, I didn't understand the question. Finally I laughed when I realized that he was saying I really had no control over what people did with what I wrote once it left my computer. I said, 'Everything in my curriculum is there for a specific purpose. Leaving something out will destroy the integrity of the whole piece.' And I believed that to be true.

"Then my editor suggested some 'what ifs:'

What if there is only forty-five minutes instead of an hour?
What if the church doesn't have a tape player?
What if the church can't afford to buy the student books?
What if there are too many students to do the game you've suggested?

"He kept going until I finally said, 'Okay. I get your point. Why do we even bother?' He reminded me that the purpose of a Sunday school teacher is not to teach a curriculum resource, it is to teach people. The resource is a tool. That is the point I would like to make with you tonight. A curriculum resource is an important tool, but it is only a tool. The minute covering the material becomes more important than ministering to those in your class, you have missed the point.

> The purpose of a teacher is not to teach curriculum, it is to teach people.

"Many teachers begin teaching without the training they need. They may even get trained on how to use curriculum resources in lieu of being trained to teach. It is easier to tell someone how to follow the step-by-step directions included in most resources, than it is to help someone understand how to teach people. As much as I want to encourage you to use curriculum resources as the basis of anything you do in Sunday school, it is equally important that you recognize your role as being more than a slave to a process.

"I would like you to look at the screen for a working definition of curriculum: Curriculum is all of the elements that are a part of the educational plan in a particular setting or experience."

> Curriculum is all of the elements that are a part of the educational plan in a particular setting or experience.

"This definition is important. It is the reason that I have been careful to call the traditionally printed material curriculum resources. They are a resource or tool for you to accomplish your goals with the group you are teaching. Can anyone think of other elements of the curriculum we use?"

"What about the posters on the wall in my classroom?"

"Maybe the way our youth room is painted to reflect who youth are in our community of faith?"

"The version of the Bible we use to read scripture?"

"And those songs we play as the children are coming through the door."

"You are all right. Basically, anything that affects the overall experience and communicates a message to your students is curriculum. Because of the broad nature of curriculum, we do need to be intentional about how we use it all to fulfill our purpose in the Sunday school.

"The first question about how to use curriculum is related to what you want to accomplish in your class. If you are looking for a more holistic approach, many denominational publishers provide dated materials that relate to the church year, and cover a set of themes or a portion of the Bible in a set time frame. These resources tend to be more general in nature, and more of a challenge if you are trying to adapt them to your own themes.

"There is also a myriad selection of themed curriculum available from denominational and independent publishers. If you know what you want to study and for how long, you can probably find a curriculum resource to help you with almost any theme. These resources will still probably require some adaptation. I'm not sure I've ever used curriculum exactly the way I wrote it."

A man on the right side of the crowd was almost standing up waving his hand. "I have a question."

"Feel free to ask it," responded Tom.

"When I've tried to use some of that independent curriculum, it looks exciting in the store, so I buy it. Then I get it home and start working on my Sunday school lesson and realize that it says something about the Bible, or God, or Jesus that I just can't agree with. Then I just have to start over. Is it safest to just use the curriculum we can get from our own denomination?"

"A lot of people have had the same experience with curriculum from sources other than their own denomination. Actually, sometimes we even have differences with how people in our own denomination write. I would suggest that you review the curriculum before you buy it, or check out the return policy before you order it. Make sure you can agree with enough of the theology and philosophy that it is useable for your class. As I said earlier, we all have to make adjustments to curriculum, we just need to decide how much we are willing to make. We also need to be sure we are comfortable accepting theological assumptions that provide the foundation for the curriculum resource. This may be a place where you need the expertise of your pastor, who has been trained in seminary to recognize theological and philosophical nuances that a layperson might miss. While you may be hesitant to ask for his or her help, most pastors are excited about utilizing what they learned in seminary for practical purposes.

"Pay special attention to what the curriculum says about the Bible, God, Jesus, and the nature of people. If what you read doesn't agree with what you believe and what your pastor preaches, it probably is a good idea to continue looking."

A woman in the group spoke up. "You know, I think it's easier to do my own thing than it is to figure that all out."

"That may be true. If you decide to create your own curriculum—because that really is what you are doing—consider these steps:

1) Decide on topics for a specific period of time.

2) Include others in the planning to assure differences in points of view.

3) Compare plans each week to be sure you are using a variety of educational opportunities.

4) Let your pastor take a look, just to make sure everything fits with your goals for Sunday school as a church.

5) Refer to your list of topics in the future so you don't repeat yourself.

"There's something appealing to the idea of developing your own curriculum. In some situations, it may end up being your best option. The risk you run is that you are missing out on the experience, research, theological perspective, educational understandings, and writing skills of those who create curriculum resources as a profession. Another question would be, what you are missing out on while you are writing? Could your time be better invested in other ways of enriching your class? These are just some things for you to think about as you make that decision. It is often easier to adapt something that is already written, than to create your own curriculum resources from scratch.

"My time is almost up, and I sense that others of you might have questions. I would like to do a couple of things. One is to let you know that I'll hang around here afterwards, for as long as any of you would like, to discuss issues related to curriculum. The other is to suggest a great resource for a more in-depth discussion of curriculum, utilizing curriculum resources, and evaluating curriculum resources for use in your setting. The resource is chapter nine, "Choosing Curriculum Resources" in the workbook *The Ministry of Christian Education and Formation: A Practical Guide for your Congregation* [Diana Hynson, et. al., (Nashville: Discipleship Resources)]."

"Tom, thank you so much for being with us tonight. I am sure that your input has been valuable." Linda said. "I want to invite everyone to squeeze together to form a circle around the room for a closing time of prayer.

"Oh God, we know that you have loved us even before our bodies were formed in our mother's womb. We know that each of us is special and important to you. As we seek to serve you through the Sunday school in so many ways in so many places, gladden our hearts and strengthen our determinations. May we see more and more of your children of all ages come to a meaningful relationship with you in Sunday school classes throughout the area. Allow us to build on the foundation of Christian community that has emerged from our needs, and enable us to truly become your church without walls and boundaries. Amen."

The "amen" was echoed around the room as new friends spent time talking and comparing notes. These eight months had indeed begun a new era in the community, and people were anxious that it not falter.

Thoughts Along the Path

What has your experience been when you have used denominational curriculum?

Have you ever used curriculum from an independent publisher? How did it work?

Have you ever tried to "do your own thing?" Did you feel that your students got as much out of it as when you used published curriculum resources? Why or why not?

14

The Future Is Now

Mark and Robert were running around outside the church. They had just finished walking a labyrinth as a part of a Sunday school session focusing on hearing God speak. It had been a very cool experience. They had never had a class that was in total silence before, but as soon as the woman who was in the chapel with the labyrinth explained how this was a very old way of connecting with God, and that you walked the labyrinth in silence, everybody just got quiet. Randy and Susan sped through and were back out before most people even started, but even they were quiet while everyone had time to walk the path.

This was a very different Sunday school experience for both Mark and Robert, and they were comparing their experiences as they wandered around the church property while waiting for their parents.

"It felt like God was right there walking beside me," said Mark.

"Well, I thought someone was right there in the center with me. I just wanted to stay and enjoy the warmth. It's really cool how our teachers are always finding new ways for us to experience God," Robert commented.

"Yeah, Sunday school was okay before, but my parents say that after most of our teachers went to some seminar or something they came back with lots of new ideas." Robert reflected.

"Well, I don't know what happened, but it sure beats sitting in chairs for the whole hour with Mr. Jackson yelling at Randy and Susan for tickling the back of my neck," responded Mark.

"Yeah, I'm glad my parents chose a church that makes the God-stuff fun. You think we can run all the way around the building before they come looking for us?" challenged Robert.

"Just try to catch me!" And Mark was out of sight.

Sunday school was over for the morning, the students and teachers were all gone, and everything was quiet in the education wing at St. Andrews. Linda walked quietly through the halls, stopping occasionally to peer into a room and remember the life that had filled the space just a few minutes earlier. She had invested a lot of time and energy into the group of churches who developed the series of workshops for the community. Had it been worth it?

Reports had been flowing in by phone and through e-mails, telling Linda how churches in the area were going in new directions with their Sunday schools. The communications were brimming with excitement as they told stories of new life in their Sunday schools. There were some innovative new ways of making God real to children, youth, and adults. Churches weren't just finding paths that were new to them, they were blazing new paths of their own for Sunday school in the future.

One e-mail she just received even told about a sixth grade Sunday school class that had a tremendously moving experience using a labyrinth in silence for most of their Sunday school hour!

Surely this sacred challenge had been worth every ounce of effort.

Thoughts Along the Path

Throughout *Sacred Challenge: Blazing a New Path for the Sunday School of the Future*, you have been encouraged to consider the strengths of your current Sunday school ministry, and look at possibilities for building on those to create a new Sunday school that meets current and future challenges.

What are you now thinking about the potential of your Sunday school for the future?

What will you do to help transform the future of your Sunday school?

How can you see God working through this process to create new growth in your life?

Appendix:
Sunday School
Effectiveness
Assessment

What are the attendance numbers for the past five years in your
Sunday school?

	Year 1	Year 2	Year 3	Year 4	Year 5
Childern					
Youth					
Adults					
Leaders					
Total					

What can you learn from the trends you see?

Has your Sunday grown? In what areas?

Has your Sunday school stayed the same? (Within +or - 10% each year)

Has your Sunday school declined? (Greater than 10% in any year?)

Are there factors that might have influenced the trends you have experienced? What were they? How did they affect your Sunday school?
___Membership growth or decline?

___Change in community?

___Change in pastor or staff?

___Change in the way you do Sunday school?

___Change in number or style of classes offered?

What is your assessment of your Sunday school in relation to attendance information?

Do you have a Theme/Focus for your Sunday school?

What do you and the leadership of your Sunday school see as the purpose of Sunday school in your church setting?

What feedback do you get from members of the congregation in relation to your Sunday school?

	Involved	Not Currently Involved
Adults		
Youth		
Children		

What did you hear about the experiences of those you interviewed that reflected the purpose you understand for the Sunday school in your setting? (Positive or negative)

What did you hear that reflected something different about their experience? (Positive or negative)

Considering these responses, what would you see as the challenges of the Sunday school in your setting?

What are the clear strengths?

Using the Appreciative Inquiry process (see Chapter Six for more detail), what would be the strength that you feel your church should build on to effect positive change in your Sunday school?

As you look at this identified strength, what would your collective dream for the Sunday school of the future be in your situation? (Choose a time-frame and describe what Sunday school would be like if this strength is enhanced to realize your envisioned dream.)

Who are the people and groups in your organization that should be involved in order to make this dream a reality?

What changes in the way you currently do this ministry would be necessary if you are to re-invent the Sunday school in your situation to reflect this dream?

Develop a step-by-step process to move from where you are to the accomplishment of your dream.

This process may be used to move into the future in a particular area of your Sunday school ministry, to create change in several areas in a process or simultaneously, or as a way of completely reframing the way that Sunday school happens in your particular situation.